how to find true love

how to find true love

Unlock Your Romantic Flow and Create Lasting Relationships

FRANCESCA HOGI

balance

New York Boston

Balance

Hachette Book Group

1290 Avenue of the Americas

New York, NY 10104

GCP-Balance.com

@GCPBalance

First Edition: April 2025

Balance is an imprint of Grand Central Publishing. The Balance name and logo are registered trademarks of Hachette Book Group, Inc.

The publisher is not responsible for websites (or their content) that are not owned by the publisher.

The Hachette Speakers Bureau provides a wide range of authors for speaking events. To find out more, go to hachettespeakersbureau.com or email HachetteSpeakers@hbgusa.com.

Balance books may be purchased in bulk for business, educational, or promotional use. For information, please contact your local bookseller or the Hachette Book Group Special Markets Department at special.markets@hbgusa.com.

Print book interior design by Marie Mundaca

Library of Congress Cataloging-in-Publication Data

Names: Hogi, Francesca, author.

Title: How to find true love : unlock your romantic flow and create lasting relationships / Francesca Hogi.

Description: First edition. | New York : Balance, 2025.

Identifiers: LCCN 2024047458 | ISBN 9781538769577 (hardcover) | ISBN 9781538769591 (ebook)

Subjects: LCSH: Dating (Social customs) | Love. | Mate selection.

Classification: LCC HQ801 .H676 2025 | DDC 646.7/7—dc23/eng/20241211

LC record available at https://lccn.loc.gov/2024047458

ISBNs: 9781538769577 (hardcover), 9781538769591 (ebook)

Printed in the United States of America

LSC-C

Printing 1, 2025

To you, the reader. It is my greatest wish that this book empowers and excites you to live a life full of true love, starting now.

Contents

CONTENTS

Step 3: Connect with a Higher Love (Soulset)

Step 4: Date in Alignment with Love (Skillset)

how to find true love

introduction

If you feel disempowered, skeptical, or at a loss as to whether true love even exists, much less whether you have the power to make it real in your life, who could blame you? True love can appear to be dependent on nothing but random luck and good timing.

Despite outer appearances to the contrary, you can connect to love so deeply you make true love *inevitable*. Why? Because true love is an inside job. This book is a practical guide to finding it for yourself in the age of a broken dating culture, digital overload, and an ongoing loneliness epidemic. Trust me, there is a world of romantic possibility that lies beyond dating apps, ghosting, and hookups. The power of love can take you there.

It's true that some folks seem to "stumble" into a great relationship, sometimes while not actively seeking one. This is wonderful for them, but there's more to the story. If you haven't yet met the partner with whom you'll co-create a true love relationship, it just means your path to this destination will be a bit different.

I took the scenic route to true love, with lots of detours along the way. However, one person's path is just that—an individual experience that doesn't necessarily apply to where you are on your love journey. If you've come to this book for help with your search for true love, I can offer you the love lessons and resulting process I've developed over more than a decade of helping other people find love. First as a matchmaker, now as a love coach and educator. I've spoken to and worked with thousands of singles of all backgrounds, races, genders, sexual orientations, ages, and relationship histories. From divorced after decades of marriage to never dated and everything in between, I've learned what I share in this book through the diversity of clients, students, and audiences I've interacted with.

The four parts of this book explore the four dimensions of love I focus on in my work. These steps are designed to meet you where you are, no matter where you are, and assist you to your true love destination. They are:

Step 1: Change How You Think About Love (Mindset)
Step 2: Feel Better About Love [and Yourself] (Heartset)
Step 3: Connect with a Higher Love (Soulset)
Step 4: Date in Alignment with Love (Skillset)

Dating: A Brief History

We used to be on the same page about courtship and dating. For most of human history, within our respective societies, we agreed about how relationships worked. We agreed that marriage and procreation were the primary goals of one's life, particularly for women. With that clarity came a simpler path to a "successful relationship." Here's some context on why and how we found ourselves in the current dating moment:

INTRODUCTION

- **13.8 billion years ago:** Known universe begins.
- **150,000 years ago:** Emergence of modern *Homo sapiens* (i.e., "people").
- **12,000 years ago:** The agricultural revolution begins; farms need labor, a.k.a. spouses and offspring, setting the stage for marriage to become the norm across the globe. Love is typically incidental to the realities of survival and succession.
- **Late 1600s/Early 1700s:** In Victorian England, the concept of a "companionate marriage" based on mutual affection, as well as the concept of "love at first sight," take hold. Personal ads start appearing in British newspapers, placed by bachelors seeking eligible wives.[1]
- **1727:** Englishwoman Helen Morrison makes history as the first woman to place a personal ad in a newspaper and is committed to a mental asylum for three weeks as a result.[2]
- **1800s:** Personal ads face a backlash due to the proliferation of a new type of financial scam—the romance grifter and the invention of the fake profile.
- **Late 1800s:** The Industrial Revolution begins; factories need labor, and young, unmarried people begin moving to American cities alone for the first time. Marriage is no longer predominantly dictated by family and community of origin; a new era of human mating begins with the invention of unchaperoned dating.
- **Mid 1900s:** Dating makes its way from working-class city dwellers to American suburban youth as the new middle class relocates in droves. Dating goes mainstream as

1 Ayda Loewen-Clarke, "Date Like a Victorian: Courtship and Romance in the Victorian Era," Dalnavert Museum and Visitors' Centre, February 12, 2021, https://www.friendsofdalnavert.ca/blog/2021/2/12/date-like-a-victorian-courtship-and-romance-in-the-victorian-era.
2 Susie Lee, "The History of Online Dating from 1695 to Now," Huffpost, February 14, 2016, https://www.huffpost.com/entry/timeline-online-dating-fr_b_9228040.

romance merges with the pursuit of the American dream— a house and a family of one's own.[3]

- **1950:** Disney releases *Cinderella*, a box-office smash that established the template for the fairy-tale princess, forever imprinting "happily ever after" and the "fairy-tale wedding" into popular culture.[4]
- **1959:** Happy Family Planning Services launches the first known computer-based dating service.
- **1967:** The landmark U.S. Supreme Court ruling in *Loving v. Virginia* unanimously strikes down state laws prohibiting marriage between different races. Throughout the 1960s and 1970s, the Civil Rights, Women's Liberation, Gay Rights, and other social movements dramatically alter social and romantic life in the United States and in many countries around the world.
- **1990s:** Talking to strangers on the internet becomes a mainstream thing; people immediately start "dating" in chat rooms. Match.com launches, establishing the blueprint for modern online dating.
- **2012:** Following in the footsteps of gay dating app Grindr and others, Tinder is born in the early days of the smartphone revolution, forever changing courtship and reducing attention spans by introducing the gamified feature of the "swipe."
- **2015:** "Tinder and the Dawn of the 'Dating Apocalypse'" is published in *Vanity Fair*, condemning the rise of dating apps and the "hookup culture" they enable.[5]

---

3 Moira Weigel, *Labor of Love: The Invention of Dating* (Farrar, Straus and Giroux, 2016), 45.
4 "The History, Debut, and Impact of Disney's Classic Cinderella," Walt Disney Family Museum, August 3, 2020, https://www.waltdisney.org/blog/history-debut-and -impact-disneys-classic-cinderella.
5 Nancy Jo Sales, "Tinder and the Dawn of the 'Dating Apocalypse,'" *Vanity Fair*, September 2015, https://www.vanityfair.com/culture/2015/08/tinder-hook -up-culture-end-of-dating.

- **2020:** The COVID-19 pandemic sparked a brief digital dating "renaissance" with Zoom video dates going mainstream and record numbers of dating app sign-ups.
- **2023:** Romance scams cost U.S. consumers (at least) $1.14 billion by using "love bombing" to gain victims' affection and trust on dating apps and social media platforms.[6]
- **Today:** The majority of single adults seeking relationships are burned out and frustrated by the state of modern dating culture.[7] Additionally, we're standing at the precipice of the next dating revolution, thanks to artificial intelligence (AI) and its rapidly expanding use in the dating realm. The first AI "marriage" between a human and her AI has already taken place in the United States.[8]

A New Definition of True Love

The fantasy version of true love is focused on another person, who you might consider your "one true love." In truth, there are multiple people with whom you can have a deep romantic connection. Perhaps you've already met one or more of them. If you feel regretful over your past and potential missed chances, take heart—more potential true loves will cross your path in the future (love is abundant like that). For the purposes of this book and the process you'll learn, true love is first and foremost a type of relationship.

All relationships have their own dynamics and values, and not

6 Lesley Fair, "Love Stinks"—When a Scammer Is Involved," Federal Trade Commission, February 13, 2024, https://www.ftc.gov/business-guidance/blog/2024/02/love-stinks-when-scammer-involved.

7 Kimberley Bond, "Why Does Dating Suck Right Now?," *Vice*, March 14, 2023, https://www.vice.com/en/article/93k9jd/why-dating-sucks-we-asked-experts.

8 "Woman Who 'Married' an AI Chatbot After Toxic Relationships Says It Helped Her Heal from Abuse," *South China Morning Post*, June 16, 2023, https://www.scmp.com/news/world/united-states-canada/article/3224404/woman-who-married-ai-chatbot-after-toxic-relationships-says-it-helped-her-heal-abuse.

all of your romantic connections, no matter how deep, are ready for, or are capable of, co-creating a lasting true love relationship. Understanding the characteristics of true love will help to clarify your past experiences and guide you in the future. They are:

- **Unconditional love:** More than a feeling, it's a choice to unconditionally treat each other with love, even when you disagree.
- **Unconditional respect:** Respect shouldn't have to be earned; it is the default setting for a healthy partnership.
- **Emotional intimacy:** The unique and private bond that forms due to closeness and consensual sharing of feelings.
- **Physical intimacy:** The unique and private bond that comes from closeness, privacy, and affection, sexual or otherwise.
- **Emotional safety:** Security in knowing your feelings will be honored.
- **Physical safety:** Security in knowing your physical well-being will be honored.
- **Commitment:** Without being on the same page about your status, it's difficult to trust and feel secure in your relationship.
- **Adoration:** You just really, really dig each other.
- **Joy:** Being in partnership enhances the good feelings in each other's lives.

I'm so glad you're here, and I'm excited for you to learn for yourself that true love isn't a pipe dream. No matter your romantic history, present circumstances, or dating challenges, true love is still available to you. Prepare to embrace a radically different perspective on your romantic possibility.

STEP 1

change how you think about love (mindset)

CHAPTER 1

center love

Let's begin by putting love front and center. What role do you want love to play in your life? A starring role or that of an occasional special guest? Do you want love to occupy only specific aspects of your life, like romance and family, while being absent from the rest? Or would you prefer to bring love with you wherever you go?

Love isn't something most of us were taught to embody in our lives holistically, and we don't have many role models of what a life full of love looks like. Societally, we rank love. For instance, you're expected to feel more love for your parent than your neighbor. Our cultural obsession with the power and beauty of romantic love can be seen in everything from music to advertising to works of art. You can witness it by what your relatives ask you about at a holiday dinner and by the avalanche of likes an engagement announcement gets on social media. Only parenthood (specifically motherhood) comes close. Even then, we're taught "first comes love, then comes marriage, then comes baby in a baby carriage!"

Of course, romance is why you're here reading this book, and it's why I've written it. Romantic love *is* powerful. How many other aspects of life are capable of being as relevant to your life goals at both age 16 and 60? Romance—or our ideas of it—meets us wherever we are in our lives, telling us how much we need it to be happy.

You can both prioritize calling in a true love partnership and embracing love in your life overall. These two things can coexist, and when they do, love flows more easily and freely throughout your love journey. Consider this your invitation to release any stories that say you need romantic love to be happy, or complete, or successful. You are already a living embodiment of love, and you get to tap into that love right now, regardless of your relationship status. Love can play a starring role in your life, starting now. When you combine a commitment to centering love with an intention for romantic partnership, true love becomes an organic extension of your loving choices.

Love, Love, Everywhere . . . and Yet

Despite our aspirations, romantic love too often feels inaccessible or reserved for the lucky few who can both find and keep it. For everyone else? There's not a lot of useful guidance on that front. Be a damsel in distress? Be a knight in shining armor? Kiss all the frogs? Finding the love you want that also matches what you've been told about love can feel like an impossible task.

When the world insists that romance is the pinnacle of love, the goal of falling in love can carry the weight of all your hopes and dreams. Not only does this put unhelpful pressure on you to even begin the process of meeting your person, but it can also make you feel like you're failing at life if you're less than blissfully happy with your *One True Love*. Does this paradigm feel like a setup? It absolutely is. The scarcity mindset reflected by our win/lose thinking about love is ultimately based in fear. How can we manifest romantic love from its complete opposite?

CENTER LOVE

We've all experienced some degree of romantic struggle, and if you're lucky, its opposite—romantic flow. Psychology defines a flow state as being so engrossed in an activity that time and distraction all fall away. Athletes refer to this elevated state as "the zone." My definition of romantic flow isn't one of a constant, laser focus on your love life. On the contrary, romantic flow is more like cruise control in a car. You've set the destination, and now you're allowing the car to do the heavy lifting to get you there. You can take control at any time. You're still in the driver's seat, and you're still required to pay attention in order to arrive safely. However, gripping the wheel or accelerating and braking wildly isn't necessary. Romantic flow lies in the ability to treat your intention for true love as a destination you've predetermined in your life's journey. If you can get even a little bit closer to the place where your certainty in true love is as strong as your certainty in your GPS, romantic flow will begin to manifest in your dating and relationships. Of course, love isn't as simple as a fixed point on the map—it's not like driving to Cleveland. If you want to live a life full of love, true love is a place within you that you must repeatedly choose to go. This is wonderful news because you don't have to look high and low to find what is already inside of you. Romantic flow will inevitably arise from removing the obstacles that are currently blocking it. You don't have to become a new person to have true love; you only have to be your fully loving self.

Love is so much more than you've been taught by fairy tales and romantic comedies. Love is not just something you feel; it's something you do. You do love because you're a vessel, or a conduit of love. How else can it be expressed in your life if not through you? The doing of love is even more powerful than the feeling of it. Only doing love can save the world, and only by doing love do you evolve to that feeling of completeness we all desire. You are the main character in the *most* epic love story—your own.

how to find true love

All Love Counts as Love

"I know I have so much to be grateful for. Great friends and family . . . I know there's a lot of love in my life. But why can't I just meet my person?" As a love coach, I hear a version of this sentiment all the time. Long before I built a career helping people succeed on their love journeys, I spent many years feeling the same about my own. It's hard not to absorb the belief that none of your other relationships matter *as much* as your romantic ones. When we cosign this view, we take our relationships, including the relationship with ourselves, for granted.

Romantic love is touted as the "best" love, the "ultimate" love, the love that matters most. Self-love is nice to have but is not the focus. Friends are great, but they won't save you from dying alone. That's the message we receive from the fear-based culture we occupy. Buoyed by fear, up on its lofty pedestal, is romance. Your salvation. And yet, you've been told countless times it's "out there" *somewhere*, like the perfect pair of jeans. Boldly seek it out or sit idly by, waiting for it to come into your life. Conventional wisdom around romance is: *If it happens, it happens when it happens. And you're failing every moment it isn't happening.* Whew. What an *unloving* pressure (fear) to instill in our psyches around love.

Maybe a different approach is needed. You can choose to abolish mental love hierarchies and embrace all love as equally meaningful. Love feels far away when it only occupies corners, or slices of life. Many clients come to me with the expectation that romantic love should be so big, so all-encompassing, that it should make up for the parts of their lives where love is absent or neglected.

A more holistic approach to love is truer to love's power. What I coach my clients on, and what I hope to teach you, too, is to place love at the center of your life. Move it from "out there" to right here, right now. Would you prefer to feel that your romantic destiny is within your power, or would you rather it be dependent on random outside forces? Feeling powerless in love manifests as romantic love blocks—obstacles that close your heart, preventing you from letting love in. The only reliable path I've discovered to true love is the holistic one, in which you bring your loving self to your platonic friendships, your family relationships, and to whichever other communities you belong. Centering love starts with developing a true love relationship with yourself, first and foremost. Honor the truth that wherever you go, love goes. Seeing yourself as the unique expression of love that you truly are connects you to it in a powerful, unflinching way.

None of this is to suggest you shouldn't prioritize seeking a romantic partner, if that's what you desire. I am a love coach, after all, and you're here because a romantic partnership is what you want. My own romantic partnership makes my heart sing every day. But if you think being single means you have no "love life," you've constructed a barrier to having true love in the first place. This mindset sneakily gaslights you into thinking you have no direct connection to love or responsibility to grow in love. Love can't feel far away and accessible at the same time. The more love you cultivate overall throughout your life, the more romantic love becomes a natural extension of the energy you already embody.

Harness the Power of Love Inside You

Imagine a wagon wheel, with all its spokes symmetrically convening at one center hub. Now imagine that wheel represents your life. That hub in the center? That's you, as love—the real you, the one who was born unpolluted by fear. You started there, from that worthy place when you showed up on this planet. In the wheel of your life, each spoke represents a different aspect, from family to friendships to career to money to body, romance, etc. All relationships branch out from the loving core that is you.

This is all very good news, and my intention is that you know in your heart the truth of your power by the time you're done reading this book. It doesn't mean that your traumas or hardships are irrelevant; they most definitely are not. Life doesn't exist in a vacuum where we can stay grounded in the safety of unconditional love, sheltered from the world. Your experiences matter, but they are not your destiny. I argue that the love journey is the whole point of being human. Becoming *more* loving—not only in feeling but also in doing—is how you embody/become the loving being that is your birthright.

If I ask you to conjure the image of a person who successfully embodies the energy of love, it's unlikely to include someone who loves their spouse deeply and hates everyone and everything else. You probably imagine someone who brings love in their interactions and to the world around them generally. Being more loving doesn't mean you have to walk through the world trying to make friends with everyone (but it might if that's your authentic personality). Centering love isn't about being extroverted or outgoing; everyone can choose love in countless ways.

Understand Romantic Love

Over a decade ago, I left a career as an attorney to do what many in my life thought was a whim—help people find great partners and build lasting relationships. In truth, I was naïve about love at the beginning. Like so many, I believed that a great relationship was primarily about meeting The One, or at least one of the potential Ones out there, and making a commitment to share a life together. When I embarked on my career as a professional matchmaker, I was focused on delivering to my clients the kinds of partners they were asking for. That was my idea of success.

It didn't take long for me to realize that love wasn't that simple. What people want in a partner is not always what they *need*, or even what exists! Finding the professionally successful, good-looking, and relationship-minded matches my clients wanted was hard work. But that was the job I signed up for, and I devoted myself to the task. However, it soon became apparent that getting what you asked for out loud could not override an inner absence of love. The clients I could successfully match took responsibility for their actions in love. The ones who thought they could outsource the work of *doing* love without personal responsibility for how they were showing up? They were hard to work with and quick to project their frustrations onto others.

Romance will not save you from a life disconnected from love. Falling in love is the beginning; staying in love is unlikely to happen if your only knowledge of love is fleeting *feelings* of it. Most people are chasing the feelings of love via sexual chemistry and happy brain chemicals like dopamine. Feeling love consistently only comes from a commitment to consistently *being* loving.

The Love to Fear Spectrum

The opposite of love is fear. You can plot every single human emotion, relationship, experience, and decision on the fluctuating continuum of love to fear. Hate, which we're told is love's opposite, is actually an energy and a "location" on the fear end of this spectrum. From this perspective, we can intuitively feel when we're more rooted in love or in fear.

For example, if I asked you to place creativity, joy, and acceptance on this continuum, you probably wouldn't choose the fear end. And you don't need me to tell you that jealousy, scarcity, and violence aren't compatible with the energy of love. None of this is to say you must eradicate fear to obtain true love. Fear is part of being human, and I do not advocate or believe in being afraid of being afraid. What I am now urging you to do is assess where most of your romantic energy sits on this spectrum. For most people, it's a mix of love and fear, which explains the ping-ponging of those energies that's so common in romance. Split or divided romantic energy within you causes an inner conflict that always produces chaotic and often painful results. We are genius at blocking love without even knowing why (much less how) we're doing it.

None of this is your fault. The fact is, our current romantic culture gives lip service to love but is in fact dominated by fear. The fear of, in, and around dating can be so strong that some opt out entirely, despite wanting romantic partnership. Commonly, the fear of being hurt, rejected, not good enough, losing love, or never finding it at all are at the forefront of many people's minds.

Perfection is never required for love; love itself is the perfection. I'm not saying it's impossible to manifest true love from fear, but I can assure you it won't be easy. True love certainly won't be an inevitable outcome of your dating efforts. You can "get lucky" with any mindset—but why not try one that feels good? Fear begets more fear, but luckily love is infinitely more powerful.

Plant Your Flag on the Side of Love

As a starting point in your renewed commitment to love, there are three questions you can ask yourself. Returning to the wagon wheel analogy, you can ask this about all of your "spokes," but let us begin with romantic love:

1. Where am I standing right now on this spectrum?
2. Which direction am I facing?
3. Where do I choose to plant my flag?

Where am I standing?

Given our seemingly innate negativity bias and a romantic culture saturated by fear, it is very normal to experience fear to varying degrees.

This is not a problem—it is an opportunity. Honestly answering this question is a very loving thing to do for yourself, and it's the first step in transcending whatever might be blocking you from more love.

Which direction am I facing?

Wherever you might be at this moment is a result, or manifestation, of what's come before now. This is a powerful question, because it's where you can bring the most change in the fastest time. For instance, if you see that you're in a predominantly fearful, or even a neutral, place, you can choose right now to pivot toward love. If you're on the love end, you can still intentionally choose to go deeper into love. Don't worry yet about how to move forward—this choice is the first step in aligning yourself with the energy of love.

Where do I choose to plant my flag?

This is where you activate the power of intention. I challenge you to pick a side—your whole life transforms with a commitment to the love end of the spectrum. Even if you've been standing firmly in fear up until now, you start to transcend it by making this choice. Just like when you put an address into your GPS, you know that regardless of your current location, when you pick a destination, that's where you're headed. So it goes for planting your flag, or "dropping your pin" on the side of love. Love can be your North Star. The place you can always reroute to, no matter how many detours you might take.

Committing to Love

You are a born love genius. These are words I delivered in my TED Talk about true love in April of 2023. I believe the truth of this sentiment; no one had to sit you down and explain to you what love is, what it feels like, or why it's important. You had to learn how to walk, talk, read, and do countless other essential things, but not how to love. That's the part we are born knowing. As we grow up, learning about love through familial example, societal osmosis, and pervasive marketing of what love should look like, the connection can grow a bit fuzzy and confused.

Usually, that confusion leads to the crapshoot approach to true love—following what society tells you and hoping to get lucky. I invite you to commit to love, and to accept at least (for now) the possibility that this commitment is the precursor to all your heart desires.

Recognize Love's Imposters

Throughout the book, I'll address many of the reasons why you might feel skeptical about love, and how to practically pivot in the direction of love as I advocate here. Love is more than words of affection or feelings of attraction and excitement. Some of the imposters that people present as love, but aren't, are common and pervasive enough to summarize here.

#1: Love vs. Infatuation

Someone recently asked me, "How do you know when you're in love?" This is a deceptively complex and important question. Love is spiritual, and falling in love is the experience of your spirit, your body, your mind, and your heart being activated and elevated.

When you're really in love, a deep connection to the love inside of you opens up. You have energy, enthusiasm, and inspiration for the one you love, as well as for love itself. When you truly love someone, you understand self-sacrifice, such as being willing to "set them free" if that's what is for their highest good. Your heart wants to treat them with love, and that means wanting what is best for them.

By contrast, infatuation can be an aspect of love, but if there's no spirit involved, it's not being "in love." When you're infatuated, your attraction, emotion, and energy is directed at this one person, which feels like love. However, you're also mentally fixated on the idea of them. It feels like they are your one and only portal to these intense feelings. In this state, it's easy to project all sorts of fantasies on them. For instance, an adolescent rite of passage is to become infatuated with a celebrity who you do not know and will likely never meet, much less have a relationship with (mine was Michael Jackson). On the extreme end of infatuation, obsession develops, which might come across as love but is actually fear in disguise. The fear is: *I can't lose this person; I can't be without this person; I have to make this person love me (or else I can't know love)*.

Understanding this distinction can save you from a lot of confusion, heartache, and mistaking someone's intense feelings for you (or yours for them) as true love.

#2: Love Scams

To provide a concrete example of how misunderstanding love causes real harm, look to the Federal Trade Commission's (FTC) ranking of the number one consumer fraud in the U.S.: romance scams. It's the fantastical expectation of true love that romance scammers exploit to con their victims. In 2022, 70,000 people reported being taken for a median amount of $4,400.[1] Sophisticated scam operations train their workers in emotionally manipulative techniques to convince their targets *this* is the love they've been dreaming of their entire lives. And then they plant the seeds of the con, pleading for cash needed for an emergency or investment opportunity.

Besides the financial repercussions, the emotional toll of these

---

1 Emma Fletcher, "Romance Scammers' Favorite Lies Exposed," Federal Trade Commission, February 9, 2023, https://www.ftc.gov/news-events/data-visualizations/data-spotlight/2023/02/romance-scammers-favorite-lies-exposed.

scams can be devastating and long-lasting. Many victims report deep depression and ongoing mistrust of current partners based on the past trauma of being scammed. It's an unacceptably high toll for people to pay and an exceptionally cruel way to rob people of money.

#3: Love Bombing

Love bombing is the practice of overwhelming declarations of love, affection, and romantic gestures by a new love interest. Have you ever connected with someone on a dating app who proceeds to send you message after message telling you how wonderful you are, how they've been looking for someone just like you, how they can't wait for you to meet their friends, parents, etc.? That's love bombing. Even when meeting in person, love bombing happens and can include gifts, romantic dates, promises of future commitment, and professing their love for you.

Love bombing is the primary tool of the romance scammer, and it is how they win the trust of their victims. Not all love bombers are scammers, but the behavior is always concerning if lasting love is what you seek. Some people equate love bombing with the ideal way a relationship should begin. In order for their bombardment of attention, declarations of affection, and the like to work, you must believe the following:

- Grand/public gestures of affection are a sure sign of real, lasting love.
- Knowing instantly that someone's the "One" is a sign of true love.
- Words and/or gifts or gestures are more important than getting to know each other at a measured pace.

#4: Control

Many young girls are taught to endure, or even be flattered by, abusive behavior by male classmates—many of us have heard, "He's doing that because he likes you," and unfortunately many brilliant adults carry the same rationale into dating. In my work, I've often had clients tell me, "But I know they really like me" as a rationale for unwanted or disturbing behavior by someone they've recently met. Interestingly, they never say it just once. In the course of an hour-long session, as they're sharing a story of violated boundaries and/or uneasy feelings due to someone's behavior, they'll say it repeatedly. Every new example will contain the disclaimer, "But I know they really like me."

Financial, emotional, physical, and psychological abuse, gaslighting, and dishonesty are all ways that control can masquerade as love. If it doesn't feel loving, that's because it's not.

We must know what love is to recognize when it's being impersonated. In manipulative romantic scenarios, even "like" can become distorted.

There's a scene in the Martin Scorsese film *Goodfellas*, where a girlfriend of Joe Pesci's violent and impulsive character proudly tells a group of other mob girlfriends and wives of his possessiveness. "He's so jealous. If I even look at anyone else, he'll kill me." Even as she speaks, she's holding her head very still and keeps her eyes downcast with a sheepish smile on her face. Her character only appears briefly in the film, but to me, it so perfectly encapsulates the *he hurts and controls me because he loves me* narrative.

This, she clearly believes, is a flattering reflection of how strongly he feels about her. Yes, this is an extreme level of control, but isn't all jealousy? "You're mine" can be taken way too far. If you believe that control and love go hand in hand, you will always choose controlling partners. Not because it's true love, but because control has been masquerading as love for a long time in your life.

For now, reflect (with self-compassionate curiosity) on your own romantic experiences and how love bombing, infatuation, scams, or generally being lied to might have impacted how much fear you have today about opening yourself up to love.

Heartwork

Love Inventory

Centering love holistically in your life is its own reward as it renews and strengthens your inner connection to love. Choosing to do this despite any feelings to the contrary is a powerful act of self-love. Additionally, it's the key to making true love a natural extension of your embodiment of love and an activation of your intention for romantic partnership. More inner love = more outer love.

Reflect on these aspects of your life:

- Romance
- Family
- Friendship
- Health/body
- Career/work
- Spirit and/or nature

For these aspects of life (feel free to expand on this list and add any specific relationships you want to examine, such as a relationship with a current partner), please write down your answers to the following questions:

1. Where am I standing right now on the spectrum of love to fear? What are the predominant emotions I experience in this area?
2. Which way am I facing? (What's my primary/default orientation?)
3. Where will I plant my flag? Am I willing to step out on faith and choose love?
4. What is one step or perspective shift I can take toward being more loving in this area?

Don't worry about coming up with "perfect" answers. As you read the next chapters, your answers will become clearer, as will your next best steps. You're off to a great start.

CHAPTER 2

escape the fairy-tale industrial complex

Sex sells. When sex is used to, say, sell blue jeans, or light beer, or hamburgers, we notice it. No one is surprised (though they might be scandalized) by a sexually explicit TV show, music video, or fragrance ad. The very salaciousness of sex in marketing and advertising grabs our attention, and we know we are being manipulated.

Sex sells, but so does true love. From the old Disney fairy tales featuring distressed princesses being rescued by their "knight in shining armor" to diamond engagement rings that "prove" your love and eternal commitment, the fantasy of eternal, lasting love with a high-status partner (an actual prince, or at least someone who can afford to pay a princely sum for a diamond) is taught to many of us since childhood. The same childhoods in which we're inundated with marketing and advertising depicting the "hot" girl getting the guy and the rich bachelor getting the beautiful woman.

From Jane Austen novels to *The Bachelor*, we've come to expect a formulaic depiction of true love: boy meets girl, drama ensues, intense feelings are felt and obstacles arise, and eventually a defining moment of romantic commitment happens (usually a "grand gesture" made by the "boy"). Happily ever after is sealed with a kiss and, often, a picture-perfect wedding. End of story.

Sex might sell fast food and music, but no one really believes eating a burger or listening to a particular song is going to make them sexy (at least not as sexy as your favorite singer or fragrance model). Not so when it comes to the marketing of love and romance. These narratives fill in the gaps of our understanding about romantic love. We see ourselves, or at least dream of being in, that fantasy, and many of us come to expect love to follow this same linear formula.

You can look at your own life and those around you to know that this isn't how true love works. You know that in real life, a "dream" wedding doesn't guarantee a happy marriage. You've seen that sometimes, the more charming and seductive someone is in the beginning, the more they'll let you down in the end. In real life, character, consistency, and the ability to be emotionally present and available is a better indicator of long-term relationship happiness than a hand-delivered bouquet of red roses. But that doesn't stop multiple industries—from entertainment, diet and fitness, beauty, weddings, and more—from selling the fantasy ideal of love.

Some years ago, I began to describe this ubiquitous intersection of romantic fantasy and commerce as the "fairy-tale industrial complex." The fairy-tale industrial complex (TFIC) not only sells, but it also hypnotizes many into believing what love and compatibility are supposed to look like if we want *Happily Ever After*. TFIC comes for us all—women most of all, but all genders. Whether you see yourself in that fairy-tale scenario or you feel excluded from it, it's inescapable in our culture.

Examine Your Assumptions

Have you heard the joke about the two fish? One fish swims up to another and says, "Hey, how's the water?" And the second fish answers, "What's water?" That's how many of us are moving through our romantic lives, thinking the love stories that permeate our culture at every turn aren't affecting us. TFIC is indeed ubiquitous in the romantic waters in which we swim.

For the record, I love a love story as much as anyone. I'm not suggesting we can't or shouldn't tell fantasy love stories. What I am advocating, however, is that you decolonize your mind and romantic expectations and separate fact from fiction. You've probably never watched a superhero movie and thought, *I have to develop superhuman strength so my life has meaning.* But you might have compared yourself to the characters in a love story and found yourself and your own life lacking as a result.

Here are some real-life examples of love beliefs clients have traced back to specific childhood memories of fairy tales and love stories:

- A man has to be big and strong enough to easily pick up a woman in his arms.
- It's the man's job to choose the woman he wants to be with, and it's the woman's job to be desirable enough to be chosen.
- If you're unmarried or no one's in love with you, it's because you're ugly and/or evil.
- You have to get married as young as possible so you don't become a spinster.
- Gay people don't fall in love.
- If I can get "the princess" to want me, I'm a real man.
- I need a rich man to take care of me.

As it turns out, it matters which of these stories you adopt as true or false. When you see these beliefs reinforced socially, it takes a conscious effort to remain empowered and grounded in the truth that love is the perfection, not a manipulated representation of it. In chapter 6, we'll dive into your personal love narratives, but TFIC has some key talking points:

1. True love is like a fantasy, a long-awaited dream come true.
2. Happily Ever After is the state of perpetual bliss awaiting you when you find (and ideally marry) The One.
3. It's your job to be as commercially desirable, with as many romantic options as possible, to be lovable.

If TFIC had a mantra, "Love is a fantasy" would be a strong candidate. And we do love to fantasize! The escapism, the dopamine hit, the distraction from all the ways we're neglecting love...Fantasy can get out of hand and actually hold us back from the messier work of loving ourselves and navigating relationships with others. Unchecked fantasy creates what I call the "fantasy fog," where we can't see love clearly. Your mind is very good at convincing you of things that aren't actually true. Lost in the fantasy fog, you might think you're open to receiving love, when in fact you're blocking it with unrealistic expectations.

What happens when fantasy goes too far?

- **We become fearful about love.** If you believed the only way to pay your bills was to win the lottery, you'd probably have a stressful relationship with money. Same goes for your relationship with romantic love. *What if I never find it? What if I'm not good enough/special enough/attractive enough for unwavering devotion? Will I lose love once my flaws are exposed?*
- **We misread the signals.** In the fantasy, a tall man is a protector, the beautiful woman has a heart of gold, and you can tell all this right away, because "when you know, you know." In

the fog, it's easy to make assumptions based on what you hope to see, not what's really in front of you.

- **We don't evolve.** Waiting for a fantasy to materialize lets us off the hook from developing the self-awareness, love skills, and vulnerability required for true love.
- **We settle for words over actions.** If the right words or gestures are all it takes to let someone into your life, you run the risk of being manipulated, mistreated, scammed, and constantly disappointed.
- **We settle for shallow relationships.** Paradoxically, the people who claim to have the highest standards romantically often have the lowest. There's always a lot of projection at work in these dynamics. For instance, "You're hot/rich/successful and therefore you can make me happy" is a delusion that blocks many from authentically seeing each other for who they really are.

Forever in a Diamond?

If a friend were to excitedly show you their new engagement ring and it was a rock…literally a gray chunk of rock, you'd probably think that was strange. Even as they explain this rock was from the mountain trail where the couple first met. And that their fiancé/fiancée had to climb the mountain again just to retrieve it. Plus, the mountain was Mount Everest. It's a pretty romantic story, but…doesn't something feel weird about a gray rock as a symbol of love and commitment? What judgments might you place on your friend or their fiancé/fiancée for not getting a diamond?

Why do we think diamond rings are the ultimate expression of loving devotion? Because in 1948, in an effort to increase sales, De Beers, the world's biggest diamond conglomerate, released their iconic "a diamond is forever" campaign to great effect. Taking advantage of the cultural reach of Hollywood, they gave diamond jewelry to movie studios to feature in films, cementing this new market in the popular imagination.

How many disastrous engagements or marriages might have been avoided if the ring hadn't been just *so perfect*? How many marriages between people who love one another were postponed or never happened because a partner didn't have the financial means to follow De Beers's self-serving guidance of spending three months' salary on the ring? How much more personal wealth could have been built for a couple's future without going into debt for diamonds and a dream wedding?

Their famous campaign didn't just create a demand for diamonds and an expectation of giving and receiving them as an expression of love. Critically, it created an expectation that a diamond *equals* love. The bigger the diamond, the better the love.

Do You Complete Me?

There are countless examples of capitalistic romantic fantasies in literature and film, from *Pride and Prejudice* to *Gentlemen Prefer Blondes* to *Boomerang*. However, *Jerry Maguire* is a particularly interesting case study. After all, this is the film that gave us both "You complete me" and "Show me the money."

At the start of the film, Jerry, played by Tom Cruise, is a hot shot, a high-flying sports agent in love with his job, and in-love-enough with his career-driven fiancée to gamely proceed with the relationship. Dorothy, who works in accounts at the same firm, is by contrast, a self-described "oldest 26-year-old in the world." Apparently due to the fact that she's a single mom with no visible romantic prospects. Dorothy, played by Renée Zellweger, is desperate for romance and a father for her son. Dorothy sums up all we know about her son's father in one sentence: "[He was] charming and popular and not-so-nice to me—and he died."

Dorothy has no interest in the past. She is looking forward, literally. Stuck in coach in a middle seat with her puking child, Dorothy longingly eavesdrops on Jerry's recounting of his engagement story to a colleague from the comfort of their first-class seats. She is so emotionally taken by Jerry's story that her son asks her what's wrong. "First class is what's wrong. It used to be a better meal; now it's a better life." Gazing up at her fantasy dream life in first class, the scene ends with Dorothy remarking, "Whoever snagged him must be one classy lady."

I rewatched this movie recently with the same level of frustration I imagine surgeons experience while watching TV hospital dramas. *This is not how love works,* I kept saying to myself. *This movie has ruined lives!* Okay, that's perhaps a bit dramatic, but there are so many problematic events in the movie, it's worth highlighting a few to explain how TFIC warps our view of love:

"Why did you marry me?" Dorothy is portrayed as a delusional and desperate woman. Due to a series of events beginning with the writing and distribution to his entire company of a manic "manifesto," Jerry is fired. Going out in a blazing spectacle, he desperately pleads for just one employee to come with him as he starts a new company. Dorothy, who has already gushed to Jerry how much she loved his manifesto, volunteers on the spot.

In the elevator with their respective boxes of belongings, they're joined by an affectionate couple using American Sign Language. Dorothy instantly swoons watching them; Jerry becomes mildly interested once he notices how taken she is by this moment. One of them signs a phrase; they passionately embrace and exit the elevator.

"Wonder what he said?" Jerry remarks. Dorothy answers, "You complete me."

At this point in the movie, we have learned some key things about Jerry: He is impulsive and is, as Rod, his one remaining client, describes, "holding on by a very thin thread." He's broke because Rod has the worst deal in the NFL. He can't be alone and has a long string of past relationships where he basically tells women what they want to hear to appease them in the moment. Jerry loves to be loved. The viewer knows these things, and so does Dorothy.

Their courtship consists of Jerry drunkenly groping her once and immediately apologizing, saying, "I'm Clarence Thomas. I'm harassing you right now." (Her reply? "I may not sue.") They then sleep together the following night. This leads to a plot twist spurred by Dorothy's disappointment in a half-hearted Jerry. In a transparent effort to appease her, they get engaged. Dorothy, instantly overjoyed, is somehow convinced Jerry's lackluster "I love you too" in response to her declarations that he's The One is sufficient to marry him.

By the time even Dorothy can no longer ignore how little Jerry is into her, she demands to know why he married her. He doesn't answer, but when Rod, observing Jerry's insistence on traveling to every game rather than being home with his new wife, asks him the same question, Jerry answers: "Loyalty. She was loyal."

"I love him for the man he wants to be and for the man he almost is." Yes, this is just a movie and maybe this seems harmless. But as someone whose job it is to talk to people about love, I can tell you "falling in love with potential" is a real thing. Perhaps you can relate. It's what happens when you choose to love someone based on a fantasy you've projected onto them (the man he almost is), ignoring someone as they are today (reality), and then feeling betrayed when they fall short of your fantasy. Dorothy has gaslit herself.

how to find true love

"He better not be good-looking," Dorothy's sister warns her when Dorothy explains why she quit her stable job. It's worse than you thought, sis. It's Tom Cruise. (Side note—her sister's caution evaporates into wistful longing for her own love story. Her character's life seems to revolve around Dorothy's emotional state and discussing men in a perpetual gathering of lovelorn divorced women she hosts in her living room.)

"You had me at hello." You might not have seen *Jerry Maguire*, but you've almost certainly heard this phrase. A contextual translation of this sentiment is: I am so willing to accept the bare minimum of effort and genuine love from you that you don't have to do anything but show up. At this point in the story, Dorothy has decided to divorce Jerry. Go Dorothy! It's obvious to her he's avoiding any intimacy with her. What sets Jerry straight? Rod has a career-making moment on the football field, and *voilà*—all of Jerry's problems are solved. With offers of deals pouring in, he's rich again, and in the euphoria of his and Rod's big moment, he thinks of... Dorothy. *Now* he's ready to love her. Or so he says (but he says a lot of things—Jerry loves a monologue and a positive reaction). He has returned to the highest-status Jerry he can be, with money and success on his own terms. So naturally the audience has been primed for this happy ending; she dreamed of this moment for so long, and it's finally here. There's us—the movie audience, and also Dorothy's sister and her crowd of "divorced women," plus their newest near-inductee, the separated Dorothy. Jerry throws open the front door of her sister's house (without knocking, of course) and announces to his captive audience, "Hello. I'm here for my wife." A famous movie speech ensues as Jerry plagiarizes the deaf couple from the elevator by famously saying, "You complete me." (And lest you be too impressed that he remembered, the movie has already gone out of its way to establish Jerry remembers *everything*.)

In the classic fairy-tale ending, the dragon has been slain, the evil spell broken. The prince has finally made it to Cinderella, and the shoe fits. Hooray! The obstacles were external to the true lovers, and now they're free to live happily ever after. Romeo and Juliet didn't live to see a happy ending, but their love was "true"—it was their families occupying the role of the evil spell. In the modern fairy tale, we are confronted with the Jerry Maguires—the emotionally unavailable people-pleaser who runs from intimacy but loves a challenge and a shot at redemption. You probably don't expect an actual Prince or Princess Charming to ride up on a horse and take you away from the pain of life. But some part of you might expect a Jerry Maguire type to put you through an emotional nightmare and then magically turn into a dream.

I'm picking on this film, but all romantic comedies follow this same formula—the barriers to love are within, but a grand gesture following a moment of clarity makes it all okay. For example, at the end of *When Harry Met Sally...*, we watch Harry's aha moment when he realizes Sally's the love of his life. As a fan of that movie, I love that moment, which sets him running through the streets of Manhattan to declare his love to Sally. That movie made New Year's Eve a romantic ideal in my adolescent mind. Sally took a bit more convincing than Dorothy (Harry did not "have her at hello," though he got her there pretty quickly), but nonetheless all her previous pain evaporates in that moment. A satisfying fantasy, but not a playbook for true love. The fantasy fog is a perilous place for your heart.

Your List Doesn't Equal Love

Unrealistic romantic expectations are often reduced to the "list" of your perfect partner's traits. Back when I was still matchmaking clients, I once spoke to a 40-year-old single woman with no relationship experience and a self-admitted habit of shutting down whenever anyone showed her any romantic interest. Let's call her Harriet. Harriet is one of my favorite type of clients to work with, probably because I can relate to being a romantic late bloomer. Had she been a coaching client, we would've focused on expanding her comfort with receiving romantic attention and learning how to date.

In this case, however, Harriet wasn't looking for a coach; she wanted romantic introductions, and she had a long list of specifications. What she *wanted* was a fantasy, though in reality she needed to learn how to connect romantically and understand what compatibility really looked like for her. Some of her must-have "requirements": a straight, white man her same age; at least 6'2" with blond hair and green eyes; a minimum of $100,000 in cash savings on hand; and an annual salary of at least $250,000. I asked Harriet when the last time was that she dated someone fitting that description. *Never,* she said. When was the last time you met someone who did? *I haven't. That's why I'm talking to you.* Harriet herself was not white, had never dated anyone white, didn't have much of her own savings at all, and was of average height. I asked her: "Do you know the average American man is 5'10"? That blond hair and green eyes is a very unusual combination? These alone are very specific criteria that basically disqualify all of your likely dating options. May I ask why this is so important? How do these things relate to your future relationship?" She had no answer beyond, "That's what I want."

Suffice it to say, Harriet and I weren't a match, and I didn't work with her. But all these years later, I still remember that conversation because it was such a stark example of how we can use "fantasy as a crutch," as author bell hooks says. Hooks was referring to romantic storytelling by screenwriters, but it applies in real life too. Harriet had fixated on a collection of desired traits, but what she really wanted is what we all want—unconditional love. A loving relationship where we're seen, valued, and honored for who we are, not for what we have or do. For a myriad of reasons she didn't choose (none of us do), retreating into a story that a tall, high-status white man was going to save her from lovelessness had unconsciously manifested as a huge barrier to love. The more specific, unlike anyone you actually know, and unrelated to your day-to-day life your relationship criteria are, the more fear (control) is getting in the way of love.

Pushing Past "Perfect"

Few of us expect perfection or fantasy in our friendships, family, community, or professional relationships. However, when it comes to romance, our standards often skyrocket to the realm of "things I've never seen in reality but still insist should exist." Seeking perfection in others isn't only unrealistic, but it also reveals a lack of acceptance within yourself. It takes confidence to let yourself be seen for your beautiful imperfections. If you don't believe you're worthy of unconditional love, you won't let yourself experience it.

Holding yourself back from any romantic interaction at all, like Harriet did, is a common by-product of thinking perfection is required for love and seeing yourself as lacking in the perfect department. Since the version of "perfect" you've been sold is in service of consumerism (selling the movie ticket, the makeup, the diet pills), you'll always be served up artificial and aspirational images to long for. TFIC thrives on us not feeling quite good enough just as we are.

Rather than battle every single negative message you've been fed in an endless game of "I'm not good enough" whack-a-mole, a more effective strategy is to transcend the whole stinking pile of them. You do this by first accepting the possibility that you are the unconditional love you seek. Meaning, the world as we know it will never love you unconditionally. If you choose—yes, *choose*—to develop an unconditionally loving relationship with yourself, you've escaped the scarcity mindset of the fantasy fog.

You can decide, right now—and I hope you will—that nothing disqualifies you from the love you seek. We'll delve deeper into how to move that sentiment from your head to your heart in chapter 4, with the Self-Love Formula. For now, please know that the first step to believing the truth of your unshakeable lovability is to decolonize your mind from any sentiment to the contrary.

The Truth of Romantic Love

Do you think love is more important than a diamond ring? Would you rather have a romantic dinner out on Valentine's Day or your anniversary than have romance be a yearlong commitment between you and your partner? Do you expect a "grand gesture" as a sign of true love? As discussed in the previous chapter, following the fantasy playbook is how scammers win your trust. Of course, not all stereotypically romantic gestures or behaviors are malicious, but if you value the gesture over the quality of the relationship, you might be heading down the path of disappointment instead of true love.

You honor romantic love by releasing the fantasy projection of it. Writing your own unique love story is romantic. Grounding yourself in the reality of what you and your partner are capable of sets you up for a better love life, not a worse one. Admittedly, when you do fall in love with a truly aligned partner, it is an intense and joyous experience. All aspects of self will be activated—mind, body, heart, and soul. But the euphoria of falling in love is not self-sustaining.

There can be a false comfort in retreating to fantasy instead of stepping up to the plate to ready yourself for the love you seek. Identifying and facing where the disconnect exists between the romantic love you want and the romantic love you have isn't always easy. But it's worth it, and your future relationships deserve your growth in love.

Heartwork

Reflect on the following questions (I recommend writing your answers down):

1. What can you remember learning about love from movies, fairy tales, love songs, etc., while growing up?
2. How much have your real-life expectations of love, marriage, and "happily ever after" been influenced by TFIC?
3. Have these expectations helped you to feel more or less empowered about your own love life? In what way(s)?
4. Are there any fairy-tale ideals you're ready to release from your real-life expectations? Which one(s) and why?

CHAPTER 3

think bigger about love

With love centered in your life, and the fog of fairy tale cleared from your mind, your next task is to expand your sense of romantic possibility. You can't predict how and when you'll meet your true love, but you can strengthen your belief that you will. The first step is to expand your expectations of how love might happen for you. These days, many people equate dating with swiping on an app, and that's the extent of their openness to romantic possibility. The multi-billion-dollar digital dating industry is happy for you to outsource your romantic expectations to their algorithms, but I don't recommend that approach. Love is bigger than an algorithm or an app that profits from your *search* for love. Dating is a state of mind as much as it's an activity that happens between you and someone else. You can take your intention for true love with you wherever you go.

Your Love Adventure

You are on a lifelong love journey. It's a one-of-a-kind adventure, personally crafted just for you. All journeys provide the opportunity to experience or learn something new. No matter how much you plan and envision how it will all unfold, journeys, like life itself, are unpredictable by nature. Uncertainty can't be avoided, no matter how much we wish that romantic love predictably led to eternal bliss. If you can't accept the uncertainty of your journey, you'll seek control in obvious and subtle ways. Shutting down romantically when you want true love is an attempt to control what you feel by avoiding what you think you can't handle. More obvious attempts at control look like a futile attempt to make circumstances, emotions, and other people's behavior suit your liking. And then getting upset when they don't. Control is having an impossible list of standards for who you'll consider dating. Or holding yourself to an impossible standard to avoid the vulnerability required to open your heart.

Things start to get easier romantically when you embrace that you're supposed to be learning and growing in love throughout your life. Dating, like life, isn't here to be easy or feel great all the time. Dating isn't just about meeting someone and getting into a relationship for its own sake. It's an important precursor to a successful relationship. The true purpose of dating is to teach you the love skills you need to not only find love, but also to continue to evolve in it. You might feel uncomfortable at times on your love journey—and you should. If you lift weights every day but don't feel your muscles straining, you won't get stronger.

This isn't a call to suffer needlessly in relationships—you're always being called to a higher love, not a lower-level relationship. Learn the difference within yourself between the discomfort of growing into a higher love and the pain of feeling disconnected from it. Single or partnered, ideally an evolution of our connection to love is always taking place.

Perfection is never required, and you can always pivot if you find yourself on an unwanted path. You're being given endless chances to embody love, as well as the ability when needed to choose love again.

how to find true love

Your love adventure is filled with lessons, forks in the road, and yes— potential detours. Without understanding the larger purpose of what you're going through, you might mistake detours and scenic attractions for your destination. We make mistakes, we're messy at times, and we often misread others or ourselves. When we're paying attention, we learn and do better as we progress.

If you were handed your ideal partner on a silver platter as soon as you dreamed them up, what would you have learned about love? About how to make it last? What lessons will you learn about surrender or vulnerability if you don't put in some work to release control? All good things take effort. What's more worthy of our intention and efforts than love? When you peel back all the layers of your desires, what remains is the desire to love and be loved and to love one's very existence. That's why we want money and career success and the "perfect" body and partner—we want to love it all. That's the sense of completeness we all crave. To be complete in love, we must *be* loving.

Of course, not everyone will experience true love inside and out in this lifetime. But everyone *can*. The possibility always exists. Currently, you might be in a dating phase, a self-exploration phase, a healing phase, or a relationship phase of your love journey. Regardless of where you are, or where you've been, it all matters to your ultimate destination—a greater experience of love.

Dating and romantic relationships expose our deepest fears and insecurities. Fear can cause our hearts to close when we're convinced disappointment and heartbreak are an indictment of what's possible for us in love. Fear can make you forget that all your experiences, even (and sometimes especially) the painful ones, serve a purpose on this journey. Meeting your person (don't worry, there are multiple to choose from) isn't the end of the road. Maybe it's the end of your dating leg, but then a whole new love adventure begins. Even if and when you enter into a true love partnership and stay together for the rest of your lives, the love journey continues as long as you do.

Love is constantly showing us the degree of connection we have to it within. The pain of not experiencing love can show us its power as much as the beauty and passion of falling in love does. Whatever happens in life, you remain your own greatest connection to love. You are your *One True Love*.

Consider the possibility that the following applies to you and your love journey:

- You're doing better than you think.
- You're closer to the love you want than you know.
- You have a gold mine of love lessons *in your highest good* waiting to be unearthed.
- Everything is in perfect timing.
- When you align how you think, feel, and embody true love, the relationship you want becomes an *inevitable* outcome.

Change the Conversation

When I talk to single people about dating, they often have little to no expectation (and therefore receptivity) that they'll actually meet someone great. The more frustrated they are about their love lives, the more skepticism I'm met with at the mention of romantic flow. This is in spite of, and contrary to, their desire to fall in love with their person in peak romantic meet-cute fashion. Their limited perspective on love often shows up within seconds of our conversation. They are quick to volunteer why they're *not* dating, or why dating isn't going well, like they owe me an explanation for being single (they don't). And most commonly, they tell me all the reasons why it's hard or impossible for them to meet anyone desirable to date. Sometimes they tell me of their most recent romantic disappointment, or share their narrative about how unlikely they are to meet anyone given the dating landscape or their personal circumstances.

The common mindset about romantic possibility I observe is: "If I don't know a specific location with tons of potential singles who meet my criteria who I also know want to date me, it's going to take a miracle for me to find someone." It's the "numbers game" approach, with the modern conditioning that dating apps have fostered—the belief that quantity and pre-selecting your preferences will ensure romantic success. Uncomfortable with the uncertainty of venturing out into the world with people whose relationship status and "type" they have yet to discover, many people put blinders on to those they organically encounter.

With that outlook, no wonder so many people think romantic love is scarce. Without a doubt, the number one question singles ask me is where they should go to meet people in real life (IRL). I usually ask them: "If you were to see someone attractive or intriguing right now, what would you do?" The most common answers I hear are:

- I wouldn't do anything.
- I'd hope they talk to me.
- I might smile or say hi or try to strike up a conversation, but also I might not.
- If I ever saw anyone attractive, I'd talk to them!

There is no real-life Tinder, with a guarantee that you won't have to make yourself too vulnerable by risking an encounter with someone not available or interested. Making snap judgments about who is and who isn't a match for you is a way of avoiding intimacy, not cultivating it. Being vulnerable and brave enough to allow yourself to be surprised by how love happens is what it takes to inevitably meet someone right for you. And yes, that vulnerability begins now.

Opening yourself up is a requirement for true love, not an optional inconvenience.

When you're single and don't want to be, it's easy to feel powerless to meet someone available, compatible, and desirable. The more this sense of powerlessness goes unchecked, the more of a block it becomes to getting the love you want. At this moment in time when there is so much cynicism and frustration about romantic relationships, you have to make a conscious decision to transcend that energy. Remember that once your intention to have true love is set, you've activated your inner GPS. But it's still up to you to unlock your cruise control and avoid slamming on the brakes, especially when romantic flow is buried under layers of fear. Something has to shift inside of you to reach a different destination in your love life. While it's understandable that dating is in the doghouse (especially dating apps), we have to start having conversations about romance that don't reinforce our biggest fears. What you focus on expands, as the saying goes, and by focusing only on how terrible and hopeless dating is, more of that same energy is manifested in people's hearts, minds, and experiences.

On social media, there are entire accounts dedicated to venting about terrible dating experiences. Yes, it's fun to share screenshots of horrible dating app profiles and rude DMs, but is that fun making you feel excited and optimistic about dating? The culture of dating won't change without a major pivot from fear to love. If you've been hovering on the fear end of the spectrum, the same goes for how you personally think, feel, and speak about what's possible for you.

The great news is, not even living in a fearful dating culture can keep you from meeting someone great, and more likely multiple someone greats. There are just some things that are beyond our human ability to thwart; love and gravity win in the end. However, accepting your fears as your reality will push love away. It breaks my heart when people tell me they've given up on dating, or even the hope of ever meeting someone. Not because they've authentically chosen to be single, but because they've been too demoralized by their experiences to dare to hope for more. If you can relate, keep reading!

Embrace the Meet-Cute Mindset

Technically speaking, you don't have to "date" to manifest true love, but you do have to be receptive enough to recognize when a romantic possibility comes along. When a couple meets the "old-fashioned way" such as in a college classroom, on a city bus, or at a dinner party, were they "dating" or were they moving through life with a certain openness to connection, plus a dash of serendipity?

No matter how hopeless it feels, I promise you there are people in this world you'd love to meet, they'd love to meet you, and it's within your power to connect with them. However, your participation is required. Your thoughts, beliefs, and assumptions are powerful, so aligning your mindset with what you want to experience is hugely important. While I was hard on romantic comedies in the previous chapter, I love how they model the myriad unexpected ways couples might meet. That part of the story isn't unrealistic, because wherever there are humans the possibility of connection exists.

To teach my clients how to embody this everyday receptivity to connection, I developed what I call the meet-cute mindset (MCM). It's a call to rise above the circumstances you find yourself in personally and culturally into the realm of unlimited love and possibility.

MCM Pillar #1: *Every time I leave the house, I have the potential to meet someone special.*

This is *the* mantra of the MCM, and I invite you to adopt it right away. I said these very words to myself over and over as an experiment in meeting cute. Back before streaming, when it aired on Sunday nights, people had a lot of criticism of *Sex and the City*—many valid—but I was focused on one: the sheer volume of men the characters met. One day I heard myself say, "It's so unrealistic how easily they meet men! Every time they leave the house, they meet someone!" This was a sticking point for me, and one day my exasperation hit a fever pitch. "Ugh! This show! I live in New York City and I never meet anyone." Which was technically true at the time, but also . . . I couldn't help but think of the friends who I'd witnessed effortlessly meeting people in all sorts of places. Finally, it occurred to me that maybe I wasn't just terminally unapproachable or unlucky. Wondering if perhaps I should be more receptive to the idea, I chose this mantra as the words I'd use to motivate me into a new perspective.

I'm happy to report a nearly 100 percent success rate when adopting an MCM, and especially of this mantra. Yes, many people are glued to their phone screens while in public spaces, but you don't have to be one of them. Look up and notice those who do the same (if only occasionally). Of the hundreds, if not thousands of clients and advice seekers I've coached on this, I consistently hear reports of at least one or two experiences of an unexpected encounter of the kind they'd never experienced before. This is regardless of where they live, how old they are, their body type, or the color of their skin. "I was walking down the street and I realized this really attractive woman was checking me out. I couldn't believe it! Once I realized what was happening, I stopped and struck up a conversation." And "Never in my life have I met someone on the subway until you gave me this challenge." These are real-life examples I've heard from clients.

MCM Pillar #2: *Where I go is less important than what I do when I get there.*

"I don't know where to go to meet people" is one of those *if-I-had-a-nickel* statements heard by love coaches everywhere. If you can relate to that dilemma, then you have a clear assignment ahead of you: learn how to flirt. (Whether that answer freaks you out, confuses you, or excites you, don't worry—you'll learn everything you need to know about the art of flirting in chapter 13.)

For now, take an honest look at your receptivity, or openness to romantic attention. Notice how comfortable—or not—you are with the idea of being approached, striking up a conversation, or even making eye contact with a stranger. What stories do you tell yourself about how you have to look for others to be interested, needing the perfect thing to say, or the types of people who want to date you (or not)? So what if you're not "their type"? They haven't met *you* yet! Sometimes—a lot of the time—people end up in happy partnerships with those who look different than they would have expected. The point here is, being around more people or in different environments doesn't matter if you don't know how to take advantage of being there.

The answer to the question of where to go is this: Go where you feel inspired; go where you see an opportunity to do something interesting and maybe meet new people; and, most importantly, go where you normally go but might usually have blinders on. Remember— every time you leave the house, you have the potential to meet someone special. It's fair and even smart to be strategic about new places to go, but having a location strategy without an MCM leaves too much possibility on the table.

MCM Pillar #3: *Serendipity is a force of the universe, and I can attract it with my intention, expectation, and openness to receive.*

You've experienced the magic of serendipity, when something so delightfully unexpected and (seemingly) unlikely happens. Unexpectedly running into the very friend who'd been on your mind in a huge crowd. Finding cash on the street (one of my personal specialties). Whenever and wherever you meet your true love will be, in retrospect, a moment of serendipity. You might not know the significance of this encounter at the time, but that's part of the magic of how love unfolds. Even if it's on a dating app, it will feel magical when you meet someone amazing.

You can make serendipity more likely and frequent by opening yourself up to it. The simple act of setting an intention to experience more serendipity will bring more of it to you. By noticing the serendipities that do arise, you will experience more of them. No coincidence is too small to matter, and even those unrelated (or seemingly unrelated) to romance still matter and should be acknowledged and appreciated.

A student in one of my classes was skeptical about her ability to court serendipity. It had been years since she'd been in a relationship, and she couldn't remember the last time she'd met a man organically that resulted in a date. This particular class, Romantic Activation, is all about awakening inner mojo and romantic confidence. I created a 30-day challenge to help my students normalize moving through the world with an openness to receive. One student, a single mother in her 50s, shared that she felt unsexy and had no confidence that there were men her age she could have a strong physical connection with. One day's prompt was to pretend that you'd get a million dollars if you met someone IRL to go on a date with that weekend. Inspired by the challenge, this student threw caution to the wind and struck up a conversation with an intriguing-looking man at the airport. They were on the same flight (serendipity!), and once they were airborne, he invited her to sit with him in an unoccupied seat. "It was so unlike me to say yes. And I looked a mess—no makeup, my hair a mess, wearing my comfy but not cute airplane clothes," she told me later. This openness led to a passionate love affair with some amazing sex. Meeting and spending time with him boosted her confidence and quelled her fear that she'd never feel sexy again.

Ultimately, they weren't a long-term match and ended things on good terms. And then she met someone else with an even more electric connection—because this time it was physical *and* emotional. She's now happily in the best relationship of her life.

I encourage you to set an intention to experience romantic serendipity and see how that begins to shift how you move through the world. Who do you notice? Who do you notice noticing you? How comfortable are you with being noticed? Are you able to breathe through any feelings of awkwardness and speak kindly to yourself when you're feeling fearful or resistant to being vulnerable?

MCM Pillar #4: I seize the moment and the opportunity to make someone's day with a smile and a hello, without getting in my head about how it might be received.

Embracing an MCM doesn't mean hitting on everyone you see, nor trying to befriend everyone. It's about sensing an opportunity and leaning into a moment of connection, regardless of the outcome. It's true that you can't know for certain how it will be received, but you can still allow yourself to be open and surprised by the power of human connection. When you embrace connection for its own sake, as an energy you want to draw more of to you, then you become less attached to the outcome of being friendlier and interacting with strangers. Remember—your next romantic partner is quite possibly a total stranger to you today.

MCM Pillar #5: I am grateful for the pleasant interactions I have and connections I make as I go through my day, regardless of who they are with or what the outcome is.

Gratitude, like serendipity and love, is a powerful force that we can tap into and harness for ourselves. Gratitude for the opportunity to connect with other humans cultivates more love within. In our hyperconnected digital society, loneliness and feelings of isolation are at an all-time high. In 2023, the U.S. Attorney General issued an advisory about the ongoing "epidemic of loneliness and isolation" with the advice that it can only be cured through more offline human connection.[1]

Be the change we need to see in this world—more people willing to reach out and connect with others beyond our screens. Let the knowledge that you are boosting your own skill at human connection, and the skill of those you encounter, carry and inspire you to be brave and open-minded.

MCM Pillar #6: *Instead of arguing for all the reasons why I can't meet someone organically, I choose to see love as abundant and know that the love I want is waiting for me to receive it.*

Do you ever hear yourself arguing for your own love limitations? If your perceived limitations are on trial, who are you testifying on behalf of?

Your Honor, I can confirm that my limitations are stronger than me, than love, than the universe itself.

Hopefully that wouldn't be your testimony. But when you hear yourself saying things like "No one ever approaches me" or "The kinds of people I'm interested in aren't available" or "As a _____, I'm invisible," you're testifying for what you do not want.

Love is an infinitely renewable resource inside of you and everyone else on earth. Yes, many people have closed themselves off to love and largely operate from fear instead. But you don't have to be one of them. To make true love inevitable, you can't be closed off to love or be convinced of its unlikeliness to flourish in your life. There are probably areas of your life, or instances in your past where you've faced challenges or perceived setbacks with determination

---

1 "Our Epidemic of Loneliness and Isolation," United States Department of Health and Human Services, 2023, https://www.hhs.gov/sites/default/files/surgeon-general -social-connection-advisory.pdf.

and confidence. The MCM is an invitation to do the same when it comes to romance.

MCM Pillar #7: *It Only Takes One*

It's a fair point to make that for some, their circumstances present an extra set of challenges. Geography, familial and other obligations, health, financial, or other challenges, discrimination, and more can contribute to feeling like the love odds are stacked insurmountably high against you. My response is this: The universe is far more abundant and creative than we are, and besides, it only takes one. You don't need a hundred people to date; you might not need to date even five more people before you meet your true love partner. If you're having difficulty seeing romantic possibility for yourself, set an intention to see the evidence you need. And then pay attention to how it shows up.

One of my clients has logistical challenges to even practicing the MCM. She is the primary caretaker and sole housemate of a relative with severe physical limitations, and she works a demanding job from home. Free time isn't a luxury she has much of, and she doesn't leave her house very often. And yet, she was delighted by an encounter she had at the car wash with one of the workers who was smitten with her, as well as with a workman who came to her house and flirted with her openly. For her, these small encounters were the evidence she needed that even with minimal contact with the outside world, there were still opportunities to meet people. It didn't matter that these were not love connections or people she planned to ever see again. She later told me, "Honestly, it was perfect because I don't have the bandwidth for more right now. It was nice to have those moments, and to know that when I'm ready for more, they will materialize."

Rejection Isn't Real

The biggest objection I encounter to adopting an MCM is the fear of rejection. In fact, if you were to sum up the biggest collective romantic dragon faced by everyone when it comes to love, it would be rejection. It hurts to be passed over or broken up with. And if you're broken up with in favor of someone else, as is often the case, it's exponentially more painful. Some fear being personally disappointed less than inflicting that pain on someone else. *Who ended it?* is such an appealing question when we hear of a romantic split, because, on some level, we want to know who to pity ("Oh my god, poor thing!") or vilify ("What an asshole! And right after their anniversary?").

Rejection is a story, not a fact. What's more, it's a heartbreaking one—because it's painful, and because it's not even true. Ultimately, when you classify a romantic disappointment as "rejection," you're saying "I wasn't enough." That's never true. Fundamentally, you are enough, and while you might not have been a match for what someone else is looking for, that doesn't diminish your worth. Nothing does. When I say, as I have for many years, "rejection isn't real," I say it with complete understanding that it *feels* real. And your feelings are always valid. But your feelings are not facts. You might *feel* that because this one person doesn't want to date you, no one else ever will. And yes, that person you don't want to keep seeing might feel your choice is an indictment of their inherent lovability. But that does not make it true.

As ubiquitous as the fear of rejection is, you can't afford to let it go unchecked within you. Trust me—it's sneaky and it's deeply rooted. Rejection hijacks your nervous system, which interprets being ghosted after a promising first date as dire as confronting a lion on the savanna. It is normal to feel fear, but we can't stop there, or rather we can't let our fear stop us. Love is too important, and ultimately you determine how much power rejection has over you.

Emotional Resiliency

You wouldn't fear rejection if you hadn't already experienced it. As painful as it was, you made it through. To help put this into perspective, let me share something about myself: I was a contestant on the reality television show *Survivor*, and I was the first person voted off the island. After returning for a second season to supposedly redeem my loss, I was the first person voted off, again. This all happened on national television, while I was sitting in my underwear and covered in mosquito bites, not in the privacy of my personal life. As for romantic disappointment, I've had plenty. I was both broken up with and voted off an island in the span of a month. I've spent years *feeling* not good enough to be truly loved and having a mountain of "evidence" to support that feeling. None of that was fun, but a turning point in my life was to use it as a way to find a deeper level of resiliency and self-love.

If you've been broken up with, ghosted, voted off an island, or romantically disappointed in any way, remember that you made it through. In chapter 1, we began with centering love for this very reason—the tendency a romantic disappointment has to take on a life of its own. Through the lens of rejection, you might judge your own deservingness of love. If the fear of not being good enough is keeping you from letting love in, you are rejecting yourself. You are rejecting your own desire for true love.

Emotional resiliency is a skill, one your lifelong love journey will test. We're not ever going to be immune from emotional pain—but you can develop the tools to handle it. Beginning with the first-person story you're telling; remember the difference between (a) what happened and (b) the story/lesson you've taken from what happened. It once took me years to recover from a breakup. The turning point was releasing the erroneous conclusion I'd been clinging to—that I'd blown my one chance at love.

There is no such thing as one chance at love, unless that's all you're willing to receive. As long as you live, you have the ability to give and receive love. How could there be only one? Is there only one person you could be friends with? Or be attracted to? Of course not. Love is an infinitely renewable resource. It isn't scarce. More people will show up ready to love you, I promise! Open up to see this for yourself.

It's Okay They Weren't Interested

Getting stuck on why it didn't work out, past the point of learning something productive (e.g., I wasn't honest, or I keep picking non-committal people), doesn't help you move forward. In dating, you can either focus on who *doesn't* want to be with you or who *does*. You're not for everyone and everyone isn't for you. I regularly talk to people who lament not being liked back on a dating app and wondering why. Psychologists estimate that up to 95% of our thoughts are unconscious. Expecting a potential or former romantic partner to have the self-awareness and desire to tell you why they aren't interested can be a trap you walk yourself right into. You can absolutely learn from what others say to you, but be careful. The more triggered you are by feelings of rejection, the more trouble you'll have receiving anything they say in a productive way, and the more difficult it'll be for you to be vulnerable moving forward.

You can be triggered even when the other person is trying to be kind, to say nothing of when they're not. Relationships can and often do end in bitterness and anger, and that can lead to intentionally hurtful words that won't bring you any closer to understanding "why" they're no longer interested. In most cases, moving on and doing your own self-reflection to make sense of what you've been through is the best way to receive clarity and closure. That can happen on your own, or with the assistance of a trusted loved one, coach, or therapist. If you get satisfactory closure through someone else's words, that's a cherry on top. But never forget you are the cake and the icing.

how to find true love

You're the Center of Your Own Universe

You are the hero of your own story. You absolutely should treat yourself as the main character you are. However, you aren't playing a starring role in everyone else's story. I say this with all the love in my heart: Stop being so self-centered. Most of the time you, me, and everyone else is a background extra in other people's lives. A lot of the fear of rejection is fueled by a self-consciousness that centers you in every interaction. If you're constantly thinking about what others think of you, that self-consciousness will stop you from being fully yourself.

How will the right people recognize you as a match if you're hidden away physically, emotionally, or energetically? A common regret I hear from clients who are fresh out of long-term relationships is how much of themselves they suppressed to keep peace in the relationship or to keep their partners happy. I often have to remind my clients to pay attention to whether they like someone they're newly dating, rather than focus on being liked. Being liked by the wrong people won't bring you any closer to true love. Many people blossom or transform after a breakup because they've either unleashed what they were holding back or discovered who they are for the first time. Your happiest and most fulfilling relationships will always be with those able to provide the space for your authentic expression and growth as you progress in life. There is a cost to blowing out your own candle in order to be palatable to someone else. If they don't love you for who you are, what is the point? You're both selling yourself short and cutting yourself off from more aligned matches. Everyone deserves to be their true selves—it's literally who you were born to be.

Heartwork

Don't believe an MCM can work for you? I challenge you to give it a try and see for yourself. Three steps to embracing a meet-cute mindset:

- **Accept that you don't know and *can't* know where, when, and how you will meet your person/people.** Insisting that you do is simply untrue and therefore not worth doing. Your energy is better spent doing your part to stay open and loving while taking whatever inspired action(s) are available to you.

Reflect: *Am I willing to adopt an unlimited love mindset?*

- **Set an intention to see the evidence you need to believe.** Don't know anyone your age who's dating anyone worth a damn? Think being queer in a small town means you'll be single forever? Set a sincere intention to see the evidence that nothing disqualifies you from true love. A starting point might be finding other people you can relate to in your community or even online who are in loving relationships. See that it's possible for others, and get curious about how you can open yourself up to allow new experiences that strengthen your faith in love.

Reflect: *Where can I find the evidence that love is abundant and available to me?*

- **Receive attention with openness and gratitude.** Say thank you (and mean it) to your barista. Wave at the toddler smiling at you in line. Make eye contact and smile back at the cutie on the laptop. Don't keep that compliment to yourself! Live your life embracing connection for connection's sake, challenging any mental chatter that would keep you closed to letting people in.

Reflect: *Am I ready to embrace and cultivate my ability to connect with others organically?*

CHAPTER 4

discover the joy of self-love

Your relationship with yourself is the blueprint for everything you accept, expect, and manifest in your life. That includes your romantic choices and is clearly visible in them. It might sound too obvious to mention, but in my experience most of us need the reminder *wherever you go, there you are.* And that includes how you treat yourself.

Narcissists are one of our favorite cultural punching bags, especially in the realm of romance. The "how to recognize/manage/break up with a narcissist" content pipeline is plentiful. But how does someone end up in a relationship with a selfish partner incapable of meeting their needs, as the common complaint goes? On some level, that state of deprivation would have to feel normal, or *familiar*, inside.

You can think of yourself as your own testing ground for love. How you love yourself will always be the template for your relationship with others. It would be psychologically irrational to allow someone to treat you in ways diametrically opposed to how you treat or think of yourself.

What Self-Love Is Not

High ego—for example, "I'm the best, my shit doesn't stink" energy is how self-love is usually portrayed in our culture. It's a natural extension of the "look the best, have the best, *be* the best" storyline of modern capitalism. We can spend endless hours and dollars in a nonstop frenzy to look, have, and be the best—by superficial standards.

In his book *A New Earth*[1], author Eckhart Tolle was the first to help me see that high ego ("I'm the best") and low ego ("I'm the worst") are simply two sides of the same coin. Which one shows up more in one person versus another is due to a combination of factors beyond the scope of this book. Suffice it to say, the ego is all about separation from others; you need it to know the difference between you, your sister, and a butterfly. Very helpful! But in the absence of unconditional love, the ego will race to rank your *worth* in comparison to your sister, a butterfly, and everyone else. It's all an attempt to fill the void caused by a lack of authentic self-love. Less helpful.

Once I started coaching singles, I saw the truth of this playing out daily with my clients and in myself. My clients have been my greatest teachers, and through them I could see the high/low ego flip-flop at play all over the place. I've had people flatly reject the idea of loving themselves as a precursor to true love. A client once sincerely asked me, "Can't I get into a relationship without loving myself?" The answer is yes—*a* relationship. But the quality of that relationship will mirror the amount of love you practice, and therefore feel, toward yourself.

High-Ego Love Blocks

"Oh, I love myself. I love myself too much. That's why I'm single—no one's on my level." This common sentiment might sound confident, but is it? Their love confidence—how much they believe they can

---

1   Eckhart Tolle, *A New Earth: Awakening to Your Life's Purpose* (Penguin Group, 2008).

DISCOVER THE JOY OF SELF-LOVE

have the love they want—is at rock bottom. In that void comes the ego to create more separation and less connection.

Signs high ego is blocking you:

- **Thinking you deserve more than other people.** You, like everyone, deserve unconditional love. What more is there to ask for?
- **Thinking you are better than other people.** You are so amazing—a literal miracle. And so is everyone else.
- **Putting other people down to boost yourself up/thinking of others as beneath you.** A scourge of modern dating discourse is how gleefully people demean and put each other down. No one is less than you (or anyone else); no human is trash. The way you look or think, and the amount of money in your bank account doesn't make you more or less worthy. Clearly, this does not mean that everyone deserves a role in your love story. Not everyone deserves a role in any of your storylines. But the fact remains—no human is worth less than you.

Low-Ego Love Blocks

Low ego masquerades as humility and self-deprecation. It can seem virtuous when paired with a high-service/high-work-ethic way of being. The more you do for others in an attempt to win their approval, the more easily you can co-create relationships where you're constantly feeling "just glad to be here" energy, ignoring the fact that you deserve as much attention and care as everyone else.

Signs of low-ego love blocks:

- Losing interest in someone once they start liking you.
- Deflecting or dismissing compliments.

- Being extra testy, judgmental, and argumentative in romantic relationships.
- Not asking for help when you could use it.
- Only seeking assistance and/or love from people you know will let you down (if you're being honest).
- Putting so much pressure on yourself and/or romantic partners the relationship fractures under the weight of unrealistic expectations.
- Ignoring your own needs (emotionally, physically, or otherwise) to the point of deprivation.
- Being the one who gives to and shows up for everyone else, getting little or no reciprocation in return.

Receiving assistance and support are love. Rest is love. Boundaries are love; saying no to someone or something when they're asking more than you have to give is love.

The Self-Love Formula

Once I became a matchmaker and coach, I felt compelled to codify what I'd learned about the real connection between self-love and romantic love. I've taught this "formula" to thousands of people, and most of them report feeling an immediate benefit to approaching self-love in this actionable way. The self-love formula (TSLF) contains 5 loving actions to systematically practice: self-compassion, self-worth, self-validation, self-care, and self-gratitude.

#1: Self-Compassion
Compassion, or kindness, is the first element of TSLF for one simple reason—you have to clear the fog of shame from your head before you can move forward. In other words, a lack of self-compassion will block you and keep you stuck, feeling confused and hopeless. Shame

is one of the key by-products of the fearful mindset of our dating culture. The whole concept of rejection, as we explored in the previous chapter, is based on shame. Author and shame researcher Brené Brown defines shame as "the intensely painful feeling or experience of believing that we are flawed and therefore unworthy of love and belonging."[2] Feelings of shame don't always announce themselves as directly as "I feel unworthy of love and belonging." They can be sneaky and normalized within us. That's why it's important to proactively address any lurking shame with proactive self-kindness.

In TSLF, you put self-compassion into action by making the in-the-moment choice to:

1. take a breath to interrupt any shaming thoughts/energy;
2. choose to give yourself a break so you can move on.

There's so much shame at play in modern dating that without a foundation of self-kindness, feeling badly about yourself is fairly unavoidable. Every client who has ever come to me for help breaking an unwanted dating pattern or to gain the confidence to date overall has a voice in their head telling them all the reasons why they're not good enough and/or why not to bother trying.

When the voice is particularly loud, it's often helpful to give it a name—one that captures the rudeness of what it says or how it makes you feel. One client named her shaming voice "Candace"—the name of her childhood tormentor. She'd say, "Shut up, Candace" to herself when her negative self-talk felt out of control. That simple mental trick helped her to distance herself in real time from shameful thoughts, rather than absorbing them as true or expending energy trying to override them.

What you say to and about yourself will always impact how you feel about yourself. How have you felt about yourself in the moments

2 Brené Brown, *Daring Greatly: How the Courage to Be Vulnerable Transforms the Way We Live, Love, Parent, and Lead* (Gotham Books, 2012).

when your self-talk was particularly judgmental or critical? Probably not your best. More likely, your absolute worst. How about those moments when you've given yourself an inner high five? You probably felt on top of the world. That's the power you have to impact how you approach life and love every day.

Self-compassion/kindness helps you do the following:

- Clear the "shame fog," allowing you to access your inner peace, wisdom, and strength.
- Be more loving/less critical of others.
- Release perfectionism, the impossible standard that keeps us feeling like we're never good enough.

#2: Self-Worth

If I could distill the "how" of finding true love down to one answer, it would be: Embody high self-worth. Not as easy as it sounds, given that we have a self-worth crisis in our culture. In many ways, capitalism requires us to feel unworthy. It's a lot easier to sell us things—clothes, cars, a certain brand of ketchup, literally everything—when we believe that owning or being associated with that thing makes us more worthy. More worthy of admiration, adulation, and ultimately, love. Consider: How much are your feelings of being good enough, successful, or valued influenced by the following:

- Your relationship status
- Your perceived number of romantic options
- Your appearance
- How much money you have in the bank
- Your weight or clothing size
- How attractive/successful/confident you are compared to others

- Your social media or general popularity
- General feelings of not being good enough

Envy, comparison, judgment, seeking validation, and so on are all normal human emotional experiences. However, on the love/fear spectrum we discussed in chapter 1, these low self-worth emotions are squarely on the fear end.

Culturally, there's much discussion of human "value" on the "dating market." So much, in fact, the definition of who is and who doesn't qualify as "worth" your time is an evergreen topic of conversation on social media. There you'll find a wide variety of "dating experts" discussing it, particularly those with loud opinions about what qualifies a woman as "high value" in the eyes of men.

The Oxford Dictionary definition of superficial is: *Appearing to be true, real or important until you look at it more carefully.* When you relate to yourself primarily through superficiality, you lose the depth and truth of who you really are. Surface appearances and circumstances can and do change, making them quicksand for your sense of worthiness, and for the relationships you form with others.

Picture a newborn baby, anywhere in the world. It could be your own baby, or a hypothetical one. Holding that vision, answer the question: Is this baby fully deserving of love, respect, safety, and care? Or do you need to wait and see how attractive or rich they grow up to be before deciding? If you can agree that baby is worthy from the start, what does that tell you about where worthiness comes from? If babies are born inherently worthy, then guess what? That includes you. No matter what's happened to you, no matter your real or perceived mistakes or challenges, your inherent worth doesn't actually change. Who can tell you otherwise?

With this in mind, set yourself free once and for all from confusing your insecurities with reality. You can both feel unworthy at times and still stay anchored in the truth that you are, in fact, unequivocally worthy of love. Taking self-worth off the table means making the question of "Am I good enough?" as irrelevant as "Does gravity exist?" Not only because it will make you feel better and make dating much easier (as if that weren't enough motivation), but also because the truth is, you are good enough.

Once you settle the question of where self-worth comes from, you're free to cultivate stronger feelings of your own worthiness. But you can't start by chasing the feeling, because you could be waiting a long time. Feelings can change, so hoping to feel good about yourself without doing anything differently to bolster your inner knowing of self-worth isn't a reliable path to transformation.

Self-worth is a North Star—an orientation of your mind and an active practice. The self-worth elevating process is simple:

1. Resolve to take your shameful feelings less seriously and take the question of your worth off the table.
2. Practice self-compassion in real time (remember, we started there for a reason).
3. Practice taking high-self-worth action by asking yourself, "If I truly believed I was worthy of unconditional love/ respect/inner peace/a true love partnership, what might I do next?" And act on your answer(s) when possible.
4. Every time you follow through on taking a high-self- worth action, acknowledge and celebrate yourself.

Send Love to Your Inner Child

When you think about it, your younger self, the one who had to find a way to make sense of a confusing and sometimes painful world, is a total badass. What a brilliant, resourceful, resilient rockstar you were. You made it. Somehow that little you figured out how to survive and got you here. How amazing. I am in awe of that little me. She was so much stronger than I feel as an adult some of the time.

I encourage you to take time to honor your inner child. They did the best they could, and what they did made you who you are today. That same spirit and strength lives inside of you now, and as corny or strange as it may sound, you can communicate with them/you. As awkward as it might feel at first, writing a letter or even speaking out loud to the younger you can be incredibly healing. Many of my clients experience breakthroughs in their feelings of worthiness and love after doing such an exercise.

1. How do you want to address your inner child? (I call mine "baby girl.")
2. What about them are you most proud of?
3. What about what they've done are you grateful for?
4. What's something they needed to hear at their lowest moment(s)?
5. What's something they got wrong about what they deserve or don't deserve?
6. What's something they got wrong about how love should look?

Once you have answers to these questions, write a letter to your inner child telling them how proud of them and grateful you are to them. Tell them what they needed to hear back then. Lovingly tell them the truth about love—that they've deserved it all along. Include whatever else comes to you during this exercise. It's very common for a floodgate of emotions and memories to open. Try deep breathing to aid your nervous system in processing what comes up.

how to find true love

You embody higher self-worth through action. When you take different actions, you will get different results than before. It's simple cause and effect. When you start taking higher self-worth actions in dating, the entire experience becomes more enjoyable and productive. *Now I'm getting somewhere* sums up how my clients feel when they start replacing their old ways of settling with higher worthiness standards.

The answer of what high-self-worth action looks like for you is one you'll have to feel your way into. As long as you ask yourself this question from a place of self-compassionate curiosity, you will start to get productive answers. Case in point is a former client who came to me for help with getting into a healthy relationship. She didn't list "self-worth" as one of the issues she was dealing with, but she did suspect that an on-again/off-again casual romantic relationship with a friend was taking its toll on her confidence. For over a decade, she and her "friend with benefits" fluctuated between no sex, some occasional sex, and long periods of not speaking after their periodic blowups.

When I taught her the self-love formula and this high-self-worth questioning process, it became clear to her that she'd been settling for a pale imitation of the relationship she truly wanted. Because they were in touch often and her boundaries with him were squishy at best, I gave her the challenge of asking herself to reflect on high-self-worth action before interacting with him. She had to feel her way through discovering what boundaries looked like with him for the first time. Later she reported: "At first when he'd call, I'd say something to myself like 'the high-self-worth action is to keep this call really short and not stay up FaceTiming with him until 2 a.m.' Then it was to not answer his call and shoot him a text telling him I'm going to bed. And eventually it was me ignoring his late-night calls entirely, and it progressed to calling him and asking him not to contact me. And actually meaning it."

It's safe to say we all have "self-worth issues" because we've yet to discover how to be adult humans without basing our sense of worthiness on outside validation. (Babies, on the other hand, don't have self-worth issues.) People who had your best interest at heart and also those who didn't, have told you, in countless subtle and not-so-subtle ways, that your worth was conditional. Love was conditional. Encouragement (love) might have been withheld as a form of punishment or under the guise of motivation. I'm not suggesting playing a blame game with your past (that's a surefire way to stay stuck there), but instead just accepting—it's not your fault you might not always know how much more you deserve. Everyone, including you, was and is doing the best we know how to do.

#3: Self-Validation

One of the most striking things I discovered through years of coaching is how bad many of us are at giving ourselves credit for our efforts. There's an epidemic of doing hard things and then robbing oneself of any validation for what we've attempted or achieved. Confidence is only gained by doing something hard or new, then acknowledging yourself for your efforts. This type of encouragement is intuitive when dealing with small children. You can witness in real time how much an encouraging word helps a child keep trying, even when something is hard. Imagine if, taking their first steps, a toddler falls down and then is told, "Well, you suck." Do you think that child is going to feel more or less confident in trying again?

You, too, need validation and encouragement. Especially when something feels challenging, like transcending fear and opening your heart to receive love. That's when the added confidence benefits you the most! To validate, encourage, big up, shout out, thank yourself—these are all acts of love. Make it a habit to give yourself credit where credit is due and watch your self-confidence skyrocket.

You can do a quick self-validation exercise right now by answering these questions:

1. What's something I've done that stretched me to be more courageous, bold, or vulnerable?
2. What courageous action(s) can I be proud of myself for, regardless of the outcome?
3. Am I willing to use these actions as evidence that I can have more confidence and faith in myself?
4. Repeat steps 1–3 as often as you like. You could probably make a long list if you think about it for a while. You've done a lot of hard things!

#4: Self-Care

Self-care is how you put self-love into physical action. It also happens to be a huge industry where all sorts of treatments, products, and activities are marketed under the banner of self-care. As a client recently remarked during a session, "I do all these things—hair, nails, buying designer clothes—and I always said that was self-care. But now when I think about it, a lot of that just makes me feel more pressure, like I have to do those things to be attractive enough."

Authentic self-care might include manicures and facials and working out, but that depends on how those things make you feel. What is the motivation? Are you hitting the gym to be good to your body and benefit your mental health? Or is your true motivation to be a certain size to be good enough? I'm not knocking caring about your appearance, but be clear on what self-care really is. Look at it more holistically than the superficial. There's no marketing team around healthy boundaries, getting more sleep, journaling, or spending time in nature. But that might be exactly what you need in order to feel the way you want to feel each day.

There is no one-size-fits-all self-care practice, because each of us is so unique. There are, however, some general guidelines everyone can benefit from. You can use these questions for anything in life, which of course includes your love journey.

1. How do I want to feel when I _____? (e.g., wake up in the morning, go on a date, exercise)
2. Am I doing anything that conflicts with how I want to feel?
3. What might I do differently that will assist me in feeling that way?

Example answers:

1. When I wake up in the morning, I want to feel rested and inspired for the day ahead.
2. Staying up way too late scrolling on social media and comparing myself to others.
3. I can finally commit to a peaceful bedtime routine that doesn't involve my phone.

#5: Self-Gratitude

Gratitude is a powerful tool for living a more fulfilling life. And where better to start practicing it than with the one-of-a-kind miracle that is you? When someone or something amazing shows up for/happens to you, you're grateful and excited, right? And that's how you want your partner to feel about you, right? To see, accept, and adore you as your unique and complete self.

Setting aside all the incredible things you've done (remember to celebrate and validate them as you learned in step #3) and all the blessings you have, focus on who you are. How incredible is it that there's never been, and never will be, someone exactly like you? You have qualities, perspectives, gifts, and talents that are yours alone. If your response to these words is anything along the lines of, "Well, I'm not that unique or special," I am glad you're reading this book. Now's the time to consider that you've overlooked your true amazingness.

Why does anyone ever fall in love with anyone else? No one ever said, "I'm so in love with them. They're just like a million other people

I've met." What makes you uniquely you is your secret weapon in attraction. Showing up authentically as yourself is a courageous thing to do, and it's how the right people will fall in love with you.

Heartwork

The following self-love check-in is a handy tool to reset when you're feeling challenged romantically (or otherwise), or simply as an active self-love practice. Write down your answers to the following:

#1: Self-compassion. How compassionate am I toward myself right now about where I am on my love journey? Am I willing, in this moment, to interrupt any judgment or negative self-talk so I can move forward?

#2: Self-worth. If I truly believed I was worthy of having the unconditional love I want, what might I do next?

#3: Self-validation. Regardless of any specific outcome, what about my love journey can I choose to give myself credit for right now?

#4: Self-care. How do I want to feel about love today? Is there anything I'm doing that's blocking that feeling? What can I do/stop doing to tap into that feeling?

#5: Self-gratitude. What about the unique and amazing being I am can I be grateful for right now?

Going forward, you can journal, meditate, or simply do a quick mental check-in using these steps.

STEP 2

feel better about love (heartset)

CHAPTER 5

strengthen your love confidence

Like loving yourself for who you are, the decision to let love flourish in your life is an act of courage. Looking at the world, it's easy to see how much we collectively resist love, defaulting to fear instead. We actively choose judgment over grace. Punishment over forgiveness. We extol the supposed virtue of moral superiority over others. Cynics tell us love is for suckers, as if love itself—and being loving—is the thing we should fear and reject. In her book *All About Love: New Visions*[1], bell hooks wisely points out that most of us are *unskilled* at love. Given this lack of know-how, it's no wonder we often don't know what to do with love.

Society has done you few favors in the "feeling good about love" department. Feeling or looking foolish is never comfortable. Who wants to be a sucker in love? Who among us hasn't pitied someone else for their heartache? You've been told countless times that anything short of Happily Ever After is a personal failing. And so, in love,

---

1 bell hooks, *All About Love: New Visions* (HarperCollins, 2018).

we feel this lurking insecurity—*Are they lying to me? Are they going to fall out of love? Does an unanswered text message mean I'll die alone?*

This insecurity, combined with less-than-positive romantic experiences, can grow in strength, but you are stronger. You have love on your side, at your core, and therefore love will never abandon you. Your confidence in love is assured as you connect more deeply to the power of love itself. In the previous chapters, we focused on decolonizing your view of love and bringing its true power front and center in your life and into your primary true love relationship—the one with yourself. In other words, changing how you think about true love makes experiencing it more tangible in your life.

Your love mindset is the first step, and now we move to your precious heart. The "heartset" of true love is a brave heart that is gentle with itself and confident enough to receive unconditional love from others. True love confidence is the knowledge that *you can handle love.* That's the first step in making the relationship you want inevitable. In this chapter and for the rest of Step 2, we're moving deeper into your heart, unlocking its power, and transcending its insecurities.

The Love Confidence Spectrum

FEAR ⬅——————————————————➡ *LOVE*

LOW CONFIDENCE ⬅——— *MIXED* ———➡ *HIGH* CONFIDENCE

During our first session, Diana lamented her best friends' seemingly effortless ability to get into committed relationships while she struggled with getting past a few dates with any one person. "What do you think your friends believe about relationships that you don't?" I asked her.

"I don't know . . . they just seem so *confident* that they can meet someone they really like and those people just seem to like them right away. I don't get it."

There's no absolute point where you're finally "confident enough" for love. "Perfect" confidence is not the goal, because it's not required. You get to both have your human insecurities and still have true love. In fact, that seems to be the only option. However, you and your future relationships will benefit from improving your love confidence, especially if the love you want feels far away right now.

As an exercise, imagine your love confidence on a scale of 1 to 10, with 1 representing the fear end of the spectrum, embodying the energy of "it's impossible for me to have the lasting love I want." On the love end, 10 represents the feeling of "I know the lasting love I want is mine." Where do you place right now? What level of faith do you have in your ability to navigate romantic relationships? How might raising that number by 1 impact your romantic life?

Confusion Tanks Confidence

"Just tell me what to do and I'll do it." "Why does this keep happening to me?" Being a love coach, I hear these types of statements often. Confusion is one of the biggest obstacles I see in the modern dating journey. You don't need me to tell you how unlikely you are to feel very confident and very confused at the same time. When things don't go well "out there" in dating, the lack of clear understanding about what's happening, why, and what to do about it can feel overwhelming to the point of despair. Add the proliferation of strong and myopic click-bait opinions on romance in social and traditional media, and it's hard to make sense of what's really going on.

Here's a quick check-in to develop the gift of clarity at any stage of romantic confusion:

1. Self-compassionate curiosity: Check in with myself—am I judging or shaming myself in any way about where I am

in my love life? If so, am I willing to choose self-kindness in this moment so I can move forward?*

2. What is the primary challenge I'm facing? For instance, meeting people to date, moving past casual dating into a committed relationship, an unwelcome pattern that's showing up, feeling motivated to date.

3. If this challenge is showing up to teach me something in my highest good about love, what might that be?

4. What is one step I can take to address this challenge and feel more confident going forward?

*If not, questions 2–4 won't be much help.

Humility and Self-Awareness

"*My* heart is open. It's these people I'm meeting that are the problem." If you've ever said a version of that, you are in good company. Also—with love—it's not true. It, of course, might be true you are meeting people who are not a match for you. But *they* are not the reason *you* don't have a true love relationship. Other people might have the ability to distract you, gaslight you perhaps, but never to block you from love's power.

We can't even block ourselves from feeling love—how could someone else do that for us? In dating, you will absolutely encounter closed-hearted people—in fact, they are necessarily overrepresented in the dating pool. Where else would they be? In loving long-term relationships? All living on a secluded island somewhere? No, they are here. And so are you, and if you're grounded in self-love and self-awareness, you can detect a closed, insecure heart and act accordingly. Most importantly, you can notice the ways in which you close yours and begin to choose differently.

We all close our hearts at times. Only sometimes is it a conscious, deliberate choice to hold yourself back from love. In your mind, you might be saying, *I'm doing everything I can to have the love I want,* while your heart is simultaneously saying, *I'm doing everything I can to keep myself safe from the love I want—too scary. Let's do this other thing instead and maintain the status quo.* The result of this inner conflict will always manifest in chaotic outcomes in your love life.

Rather than assume that the closed-hearted people of the world are the source of your disconnection to love, I encourage you to reclaim your power through humility and self-awareness. When meeting someone whose avoidance of love is evident, ask yourself, "What's my version of that?" This is a powerful question that can help clear your own hidden love blocks.

Things aren't always what they seem until you shift your perspective. For example, if being attracted to unavailable people—maybe they're with someone else or they can't handle their own feelings, much less yours—is your pattern, take heart. By normalizing love on the inside as you're learning to do in this book, you're also letting yourself know *true love is my new normal.* Your attractions will change as your skill at love does.

More Confidence = Less Hedging

The more your love confidence grows, the more progress you'll make toward the love direction on the spectrum, as your actions will be more inspired and aligned. You won't hold yourself back by inaction or ineffective action. I recently spoke to a young woman named Ellie who'd accepted my challenge to adopt a meet-cute mindset and be bold the next time she went out with friends. We debriefed soon thereafter, and I asked her how it went. "Terrible! I tried talking to someone and it didn't work." She went on to explain: "I saw this cute guy sitting with his friends, and I mustered up the courage to walk over to him. I interrupted their conversation to tell him my brother would really like his hat and asked him where he got it. He told me where, I said thank you, and walked away! It was so embarrassing."

It so happens that I disagree with Ellie's assessment that it went terribly or that she had anything to be embarrassed about. Also, with a bit more confidence, that entire situation could have gone down differently. There's no guarantee the end result wouldn't have been the same, but Ellie didn't do herself any favors by hedging as she did. As someone who used to be so love insecure I avoided dating for years, I can recognize "hedging" behavior when I hear it. It's what happens when you're trying to be brave and go for it, but there's a hesitation—a crisis of confidence—that holds you back from committing to the opportunity. Sort of like belly flopping off the high dive because you freaked out at the last minute. (I did that once too and I do not recommend it!)

I was extremely proud of Ellie for pushing herself way out of her comfort zone. For where she was in her love confidence journey, approaching a stranger in a bar was a big deal and something she normally wouldn't have ever attempted. Grateful for the chance to remind her of the importance of acknowledging and applauding her bravery, I congratulated her. She'd done a hard thing and was on the verge of completely negating her efforts because it didn't result in a love connection. Self-validation, I reminded her, isn't about celebrating outcomes (though that's important too); it's about acknowledging effort.

With a smidge more confidence and perspective, Ellie could have set herself up for a better outcome. In a moment of panic, she created an "excuse" to explain away her boldness in approaching the attractive stranger. She made up a direct question that wasn't a conversation starter, and she didn't genuinely care about the answer. Even if he had been interested in continuing a conversation with her, it wouldn't have been possible since she hightailed it out of there so quickly.

We all do the best we can in any given scenario—that's why I preach the gospel of self-compassion nonstop. With compassionate curiosity about how to act more effectively, here's an incomplete list of hypothetical alternate approaches Ellie could have taken:

Event: Ellie sees someone attractive or intriguing across the room.

Possibility 1—Keep it moving: She takes her time, breathing intentionally to calm her nervous system. She glances over to see if she can catch their eye. If not, then she can position herself closer to see how they respond to her presence. Was there a double take? A smile? Eye contact? If they're not responding with any interest, she can leave them alone and find someone more receptive to engage with.

Possibility 2—Draw them in: She takes her time, breathing intentionally to calm her nervous system. She glances over to see if she can catch their eye. If yes, then she can smile and look at them long enough for them to know her glance was on purpose. If she catches their eye again, a smile and a wave will signal she is open to being approached.

Possibility 3—Go for it: Ellie goes for it (because sometimes in life you must) and walks over. She discreetly leans in at an opportune moment to say: "Hi, I'm sorry to interrupt. I just wanted you to know I love your hat. It looks great on you. And I'm Ellie by the way."

Love Confidence Factors

Love confidence transcends the dating phase of your love journey. As I like to remind my clients, dating skills are love skills. Everything that makes you better at love-centered dating will also make you better at being in a love-centered relationship. Love confidence is no exception. Relationships, as you already know, are not magical cure-alls for our problems and insecurities. Happy relationships don't spring from two people mired in insecurity about the relationship lasting and thriving over time.

If you've ever experienced low love confidence while in a relationship, you know it's an anxiety-filled experience. I've heard dozens of people express their regret over not enjoying a past romance due to this very situation. In love, you repeatedly discover that wherever you go, there you are. Therefore, your level of love confidence will impact you for a lifetime.

Here's an incomplete list of factors that influence love confidence:

- Self-trust based on past relationship choices
- Quality of parent/caregiver relationships you witnessed growing up

- Quality of your own past relationships
- Resolution of your past relationship experiences
- Quality of your self-talk
- Feelings of worthiness
- Societal messaging via TFIC and dating culture in general
- Insecurities around desirability
- Lack of representation in media and storytelling of people who look like you, love like you, etc.
- Skill at meeting partners and progressing forward in relationships
- Skill at maintaining relationships over time
- Societal messaging about the dating pool (e.g., "everyone's a narcissist, all _____ are trash")
- Familial/friend pressure
- Familial/friend encouragement
- Fear of rejection, betrayal, being taken advantage of, etc.
- Being dependent on dating apps to meet people
- Trauma (Big "T" or little "t"—we all have it to some degree)
- Physical, mental, emotional, or spiritual health
- Financial and career circumstances
- Confidence in your physical appearance

Has your confidence improved in any of these areas since you began reading this book? Or has it naturally increased over time? Which resonates as something to give your attention to healing or addressing? What progress have you made that you can give yourself credit for right now? Progress isn't only limited to what happens between you and other people. Love is an inside job, and evidence of your growth can look like a kinder relationship with yourself, developing more self-awareness, or embracing a bigger sense of romantic possibility. By acknowledging and honoring your growth, you strengthen your own love superpowers.

Love Confidence Signals

The importance of your confidence can be seen in some of the common ways lower love confidence manifests in real life:

- A focus on being liked or chosen more so than how you feel about/while with the people you date
- Fear around dating being a waste of time or too emotionally risky
- Getting your hopes up prematurely and treating each romantic possibility as "make or break"
- Leading with what you *don't* want in a partner/relationship/date (e.g., "Don't contact me if you're _____" on a dating app)
- Irresistible/habitual focus on bad dating or relationship stories
- Feelings of hopelessness or despair around love
- Feeling that you've done everything you can and still love eludes you
- Bitterness/anger over being single or past relationships
- Settling for lackluster or toxic relationships
- Chasing or pining after unavailable partners (emotionally or otherwise)
- Difficulty establishing or maintaining healthy boundaries in relationships (e.g., people-pleasing, lack of self-care, love bombing, or oversharing)
- Strong identification with being single or unlucky in love (e.g., "I'm the single friend" or "I'm unlucky in love")
- Continually dating narcissistic or abusive partners

Contrast the preceding with these higher love confidence signals:

- More feelings of self-love and self-worth
- More acceptance rather than anxiety about relationships

- Feeling optimistic and empowered about one's love life
- Ease with walking away from relationships when your self-worth or safety (emotional or otherwise) is being compromised
- Better intuition about next steps and potential partner compatibility
- Willingness to take "imperfect" action toward cultivating more love in your life
- Attraction to others with high love confidence

Self-Confidence ≠ Love Confidence

"Confidence is sexy" is a universal maxim of romance. It typically refers to *self-confidence*, which is something we can intuitively sense in others. Mojo, swagger, presence, rizz...however you describe it, you know it when you *feel* it. Since we all intuitively respond to a certain confidence cocktail, it goes without saying that self-confidence is often the open secret to success in life and in love.

All that to say, self- and love confidence are relatives, but not twins. Being self-confident certainly helps your love life, but that alone doesn't make relationships easier. I work with a lot of self-confident people. At the start of my career, I was surprised by how large the gap sometimes was between their love confidence and self-confidence, and how much confusion and pain this asymmetry causes. These days, I've come to expect the discrepancy. It makes sense, when you consider the facts. They've achieved amazing things educationally, career-wise, and in terms of key personal goals. Many of them are total badass bosses, leaders, and changemakers. They've seen the other side of their hard work, which gives them the confidence to keep thriving in those areas.

The self-love formula you learned in the last chapter is a great tool for building more self- and love confidence. With self-compassion, you can observe any inner conflict without judgment or shame. With self-worth, you can consider that any struggle isn't an indictment of your inner capacity for love; it's information about what's really going on beyond the surface of your romantic outcomes. This is the good stuff, the understanding that transforms your love life. With intention, you can choose to move closer toward higher love confidence and self-confidence.

The following table illustrates a general representation of how different ends of the confidence spectrum interact in relationships. There is no absolute "high" or "low," so check in with yourself honestly to see where you land today.

CONFIDENCE SPECTRUM	Lower Love Confidence	Higher Love Confidence
Lower Self-Confidence	Internalized romantic challenges: "It's my fault—I'm not good enough/good enough at love."	Internalized/externalized focus: "I don't feel good about myself, but I can give love to someone else."
Higher Self-Confidence	Externalized romantic challenges: "It's not my fault—outside factors/people are to blame."	Internalized/externalized focus: "I am in control of my love journey, and I feel safe to give and receive love freely."

What does increased confidence look and feel like for you? What might make you feel more confident right now? How will increased self- or love confidence change how you date or show up in your relationships?

The Body Confidence/Love Confidence Connection

You absolutely do not have to look a particular way or have a specific body shape to be worthy of love, nor to attract an amazing partner. No matter how much you might see yourself as physically lacking, I promise you there are those who disagree. However, positive feedback about your appearance will fall on deaf ears if you can't see yourself as desirable first.

Though we live in an unprecedented era of lip service about body positivity and acceptance, the remnants of our body shaming culture are still with us. No matter what your body looks like, someone out there will shame you for it. Please don't join them. Take solace in the fact that another person's physical preferences are really about them, not you. Imagine being so obsessed with how you think other people's bodies should look or function that you turn into a hateful bigot or social media troll. No one wins at that level of consciousness, and so it must be transcended.

Melinda was a client who was eager to find a romantic partner but had held herself back from dating for over a decade due to a lack of body confidence. The idea of someone seeing her naked or touching her curves caused her so much anxiety she couldn't bring herself to approach any level of physical intimacy. Now in her 40s, she realized she'd never felt good in her own skin, and her past sexual experiences had never been enjoyable. For Melinda, sex had always been about pleasing her partner. By the time we began working together, she was disconnected from her body to the point she couldn't remember the last time she'd felt pleasure. Our focus became her feeling herself—literally. Her first assignment was to turn herself on sexually. She began masturbating and watching erotic videos that allowed her to connect with that neglected aspect of herself. I also challenged her to start going on walks and appreciating the miracle of her own body's movement. Through walking, she discovered that strength was a feeling she craved physically, and began lifting weights for the first time in her life. Over the following months, she joined a gym and started working out regularly. Melinda later told me, "I was so focused on wishing I had a different body that I didn't realize I could ever come close to loving my body as it is. I don't care about being skinny anymore. I just care about feeling strong and good in my own skin."

You already know that the better you feel, the more confident you feel in life. You've been trained to expect, accept, and strive to a societal ideal as a prerequisite for love. It is an act of rebellion to love yourself, and it is an act of rebellion to love your body. Loving your body is more than an emotional feeling—it's a choice. And it's a necessary starting point if you want to reach a higher level of body confidence. This is especially true if you were raised as a girl in Western culture, with physical differences, or if you're trans or gender nonconforming. In truth, everyone gets a dose of body and beauty shaming, even the cis-het men who are told their manhood lies in their height, the length of their penises, and the bulge of their muscles. Like TFIC, body shaming comes for us all.

Beauty, body preference—these are all as subjective as can be. Once, when the topic of international heartthrob Idris Elba came up with a woman I was speaking with, she said, "Eww." If that isn't proof that everyone is beautiful to someone and *eww* to someone else, I don't know what is. Even you and me, though I for one find us to be gorgeous!

Your love confidence will be improved by a more loving relationship with your looks and your body, beginning with how much you judge or criticize yourself. Set an intention to fall in love with your physical form, just as it is. To treat it (and therefore yourself) with love, just as you are. If there are things you want to change about your looks, you'll have an easier time if you approach that process from a place of love. There's zero downside to embracing your unique physical beauty, especially if you want to receive that adoration from someone else. I urge you to normalize that energy inside of you, starting now.

In the end, it's always about love and our need for love. The collective primal desire for the ultimate experience of love: unconditionally giving and receiving love back in return. When we feel unsafe or uncertain in love, the ego will rush in to fill the void. Fill that void with the love inside of you, with a higher love. The further away love feels for you, the more loving kindness I urge you to extend to yourself. Only by your inner commitment to love can you normalize giving and receiving love from others.

Heartwork

With self-compassionate curiosity, write down your answers to the following:

1. Where am I on the love confidence spectrum today?
2. Which aspect of romance do I feel the least confident in? How about the most confident?
3. What intention(s) can I set around increasing my love confidence in the areas where I feel less secure than I'd like? (e.g., *I set an intention to grow my confidence when it comes to choosing a great partner.*)
4. What's one step I can take to grow in the direction of increased confidence in this/these area(s)? What skill(s) can I cultivate/practice?
5. Where am I being overly critical or not giving myself credit in this/these area(s)?
6. How self-confident am I generally?

7. What about myself do I feel the most confident? How about the least?

8. What's one step I can take to grow in the direction of more self-confidence?

9. Am I willing to embrace love as a lifelong journey? How might that affect my love confidence and self-confidence?

CHAPTER 6

upgrade your beliefs, identity, and patterns

I'm never going to meet anyone. I'm going to be alone forever." Alice kept repeating this line as she recounted her recent breakup. The few weeks she'd spent dating Trevor had been emotionally thrilling, overwhelming, and had given her a welcome sliver of hope after what had been years of romantic frustration. She was in her mid-40s and deeply resentful that she'd never been married, which had been a goal of hers since childhood. Her anger at Trevor for ending their blossoming romance was palpable, as was her despair.

"I knew this was going to happen. I knew it was too good to be true." It was heart-wrenching to hear the pain in her voice. "You sound very committed to the conclusion that you'll be alone forever," I pointed out to her.

"Yes, I am," she replied without hesitation.

"So you're committed to being right about something that's the polar opposite of what you actually want?" I asked.

She laughed for the first time in the conversation and said, "Yeah, I see your point."

We went back and forth, with me asking questions that prompted Alice to articulate that looking at the situation as direly as possible was indeed a choice. Once she saw this, she started to back down as she considered a new perspective. I assigned her heartwork to write a list of at least 20 things she believed about love, from how relationships form, to how love works, to who gets to have it. She agreed and texted me a few days later:

"I'm halfway through this beliefs list and realized I'm just so afraid I'll never meet anyone. I've wanted a partner more than anything my whole life and at this point every new guy is just a confirmation I won't ever have love. So maybe this was the point of the exercise, but the strongest belief is I won't find love. I did listen to what you said and even I can see how my biggest fear is also my biggest love belief. Seems like a problem. Lol!"

This "problem" was a life-changing realization for Alice, and a huge blind spot for so many when it comes to love. What you believe is akin to a program running your psychological operating system. In meeting Trevor, Alice's fear had been activated throughout their relationship and ultimately validated by their breakup. Like Alice, your view of yourself and the role you occupy in your life story will always apply your "program" to what you see, do, and experience.

Understand the Power of Your Love Beliefs

All humans (you included) want to be right about what they believe more than they want to be happy. You will always find evidence to confirm your beliefs. If you resonate with Alice's experience of receiving repeated confirmation of what you do *not* want, uncover the belief underneath that pattern. Trevor did not cause Alice's belief she'd be alone forever. In retrospect, Alice admitted she'd sensed that she and

Trevor weren't on the same page about commitment from their first date. Despite this inner knowing, there was a level of Alice's awareness that chose to move forward with him in a way that ultimately confirmed her preexisting conviction that her relationships won't last. Her belief underneath the fear was a common one: *I have to prove myself and convince men to choose me.* Given that core belief, it makes perfect sense that she'd be attracted to men she'd have to try to convince to be with her. The ones who didn't need convincing? She had no interest in those men. Not until she understood why she was drawn to the opposite of what she actually wanted did she begin to transcend it.

Belief Clues from Breakups

In any breakup situation, there's always (1) what actually happened and (2) how what happened confirms your assumptions about how love/dating/relationships work. The latter—the confirmation bias we all have—is where people often jump. Your brain is trying to figure out what conclusion can be drawn from the situation.

Alice's realization that wanting love while simultaneously convincing herself she'll never have it was a major one. After that a-ha, she was able to find the meaning in her relationship with Trevor. As it turned out, their romance shattered some other unwanted love beliefs she'd had for years:

- ~~I can't meet people without dating apps~~ → She met Trevor in a bar.
- ~~Men are takers~~ → Trevor was generous and caretaking.
- ~~I'm only attracted to men who keep me guessing~~ → He was clear in his communication and proactive in making plans.
- ~~There are no men in this city I want to date~~ → When she opened up beyond dating apps, she met someone entirely new in her own neighborhood.

Now, I know that none of this changes Alice's very real disappointment and pain. In fact, from her perspective (at first), Trevor's good attributes only made it worse that the relationship didn't last. But here's the thing about that—Alice could no longer say she couldn't meet people in real life. She did it once, so was it *possible* that it could happen again? Of course. If you agree something is possible, then are you more or less open to imagining how to increase that possibility? How might Alice's view of dating change if she was no longer dependent on dating apps to meet potential partners? How might her openness to a new awareness of romantic possibility result in her meeting more people?

Alice unlocked a new level of personal power when she came to realize that by taking control of her love beliefs, she set herself free from the weight of the pessimism and negativity they brought her. Over the next month, we worked on deepening her embodiment of self-love. The shaming, critical voice that she'd assumed she had to live with began to lose its hold over her. She took a break from dating apps and accepted my challenge to embrace a meet-cute mindset. The next time she met someone who made it clear they weren't looking for a relationship, she listened and didn't go down the road she knew led to pain. A couple of months later, she surprised herself with the realization *she* didn't want to be with Trevor. "It doesn't matter how much I like him if he doesn't want what I want. I've had enough relationships like that. I guess he did me a favor, because I would've rode that train till the wheels fell off!"

Understand the Role of Fear

Once you start to see how powerfully belief shows up in our everyday actions and relationships, you will understand your own ability to harness its strength. Belief is one of the most significant factors in your decision-making, perspective, and life satisfaction. There are so many negative beliefs about dating that fear is most people's starting point when it comes to romantic love. With fear at the center of the collective dating narrative, it's no wonder that "evidence" justifying that fear grabs and dominates our attention.

The love to fear spectrum is a recurring theme in this book because it's so central to your love life. Fear is the antithesis of love. That doesn't make fear an enemy, but rather a teacher. What you fear in love is revealing of an inner obstacle to love. Love is an inside job, so these inner blocks matter more than what happens on the outside. If, for example, you strongly fear being seen for who you really are, you won't actually let anyone in who can see (and love) you for who you are. It would cause too much cognitive dissonance to do so. Unrecognized fear becomes an invisible line in the sand that says, *Do not cross.* Your mind is so adept and genius at keeping you on the "safe" side of this line, you might not be aware it even exists. Without knowing it, we can convince ourselves we see things as they truly are, when in fact we're missing the entire point. Only when you can distinguish between love and fear can you truly see reality.

In the journey of forming and maintaining a lasting partnership, these invisible lines, or internal blocks to love, become very apparent. Dating struggles, relationship challenges—these aren't random outcomes happening for no reason. Unwanted relationship patterns are showing up to put you on the path of seeing and transcending the fear that's causing them. You do that by self-compassionately acknowledging your own fears and planting your flag on the side of love. That's how you cross that invisible fear line—by stepping over it as you move toward love. It can be the tiniest baby step, but one that has the power of a giant leap. That is the act of transcending fear. Let fear exist (as if you have a choice); do not try to deny it. Let fear complain that you keep moving the goalpost, making its presence in your psyche increasingly less relevant. Fear will always come back, will do its best and loudest to get your attention, and so the new lesson begins. That is the path of your emotional and spiritual growth and evolution.

Transforming Love Beliefs

In this chapter, you'll learn how to identify your love beliefs and replace unwanted fears with a new love story. (In chapter 9, we'll also discuss this from an energetic perspective.) Lest you think this isn't possible, reflect on the many things you used to believe with all your heart that you wouldn't ever accept now. If believing made it so in reality, surely enough kids have believed in Santa Claus and the Tooth Fairy to materialize them by now. If TFIC was telling you the truth, Happily Ever After would be assured by being "rescued" by a high-status partner. You already know that's not how love works. But your mind is powerful enough to convince you that's how it *should* work. That's a level of self-delusion beyond our power to make true (like Santa Claus).

A useful exercise is to write down everything you can think of that you *no longer* believe. Maybe it's a belief about your ability in some area, or an experience you thought you couldn't have. For instance, maybe you never saw yourself as working in a particular field, and now you've made a career of it. Or you saw yourself as having an internal limit on what you could achieve, like learning a new language, only to do it one day. Taking it one step further, reflect on *how* that belief changed. Was it a definitive choice to form a new belief? Did you outgrow it over time? Did it crumble in an instant? Did you cling to it, rejecting any evidence to the contrary? With self-compassionate curiosity, your past can give you the confidence boost to know you *can* believe something brand-new.

With all the bad intel you've been given about romantic love, it's no wonder there are some "bugs in the program." Self-compassion is the key to uncovering these bugs in a productive and healing way. I've witnessed client after client have epiphanies once they realize, often for the first time, their most deeply held beliefs. "I've had more breakthroughs in this session than I have in ten years of therapy," a client once told me after discovering her love beliefs for the first time. You're incredibly strong to keep this hidden within you for so long. Superhero-with-your-own-movie-franchise-level strong. Once you witness this untapped power within, you can use it to neutralize the old and replace it with the new.

Neutralizing Negativity

From childhood to young adulthood, I clung to a belief that "boys don't like me." It ran on a loop in the background of my mind. It wasn't objectively true—I had been asked out and crushed on. But I was so strong in this belief that I put up strong energetic blinders to allowing any of that romantic attention to land within me. In a life-changing moment of grace, one day I "heard" these same words with newfound curiosity. The question *What if that's not true?* popped into my head. While I didn't know it at the time, that was a critical turning point in my love journey. I walked off the racetrack where "Boys don't like me" was a constant hum. A confidence that I never could have imagined possible for myself flourished within me as I allowed in more and more evidence that challenged my old love narrative.

Escape the power of your unwanted beliefs with the following steps to identify, neutralize, and replace them:

#1: What do I believe about love?

Write down at least 20 things you believe to be true about love. They should be ideas you feel are true about all aspects of romantic love. From finding it, keeping it, who gets to have it, what happens if you lose it—the whole story of love that you've used to explain your love life. Expected relationship dynamics, which role you need to play to have love . . . It's all part of your romantic belief system.

#2: Which beliefs apply to me and my relationships specifically?

Your list will likely reveal that there are different kinds of beliefs. Some are general, like *Men should pay on the first date*. Whereas *I have to be the one who sacrifices in relationships* is far more personal. It's these specific beliefs—the ones you formed in your unique cocktail of life experience—that will have the greatest impact on you.

#3: Is this true?

Whether you want it to be true or not (that's the next step), it's important to be aware of what you've subconsciously (and emotionally) solidified within you as fact. As Byron Katie teaches in her process The Work[1], which validated my own experience in shifting beliefs, the answer doesn't matter. Your purpose in asking yourself this isn't to be objective or logical. The point is—does this feel true for you?

#4: Do I *want* this to be true? If not, am I willing to consider the possibility that it isn't true, or that it won't always be?

This step might seem too simple to be effective, but trust me—from a tiny sliver of possibility, your new reality can emerge.

#5: If it isn't true, what might be true instead that I would prefer?

This process is not one of spiritual override where you will yourself into a new conviction overnight. I am no advocate of choosing the polar opposite belief with the aim of convincing yourself to make a

---

1 Byron Katie and Stephen Mitchell, *Loving What Is: Four Questions That Can Change Your Life* (Harmony/Rodale, 2002).

180-degree flip in a heartbeat. Instead, try approaching the belief from a new angle—one of possibility. Question your disempowering beliefs and watch them crack under the loving pressure of self-compassionate curiosity. For example, my answer to this question years ago wasn't "every boy likes me"—that's obviously not true for anyone. Instead "the right people for me will like me" was a real possibility I'd prefer and could come to fully believe.

#6: What "evidence" will help me to believe in a new possibility?

Sometimes you've got to see it to seriously believe it. If, for instance, you've previously believed *It'll take a miracle for me to meet someone*, some contrary evidence will do you a world of good. Don't try to control the universe's divine timing by jumping too many steps ahead of where you are on your journey and resolve to manifest your ideal partner tomorrow. Set yourself up to win by focusing on the evidence instead of the outcome. For example, discovering a romantic prospect in an unexpected place, even if it doesn't result in true love. The old story of *It'll take a miracle for me to meet someone* now has some new evidence to counter it. It was simply a Tuesday at the dentist's office. Not a place you'd expect miracles—not without a meet-cute mindset, at least. If it happened once there, maybe it can happen somewhere else too? (Psst—it can!) As you feel the old story crumble and a new one begin to emerge, revisit this step.

Examine Your Romantic Identity

If your love beliefs are a tree, your romantic identity manifests as its leaves. You can think of romantic identity as the role you play in the love story of your life. A palm tree isn't going to sprout oak leaves, and neither can you have a different self-identity than one aligned with your beliefs. How would you describe yourself as a main character in your love story? Always the friend, never the lover? The heartbreaker? The loyal partner? Would you prefer to play a different role?

When shifting a belief, pay attention to how it manifests in how you show up. For instance, my old romantic identity could be summed up by "always passed over/ignored." That was the "I am" statement I'd say out loud (or at least in my journal) about myself. As the belief lost its power over me, I eventually discovered a new romantic identity, one that I still possess today: *I'm always capable of having the love I want.* Seeing myself that way allows me to effortlessly act the way someone who has that identity naturally would, with a ton of love confidence. You can change your romantic identity to serve your highest good and love goals. But first, get clear on what that identity is currently.

What are your "I am" statements about love? The things you see as central to your romantic reality?

Once you have those answers, reflect on the following for each:

1. What does this identity mean about what's possible for me in love?
2. Does this identity make me feel more or less love confident?
3. If less, am I willing to set an intention to release/reframe this identity? In other words, am I willing to embrace a more empowered way of seeing myself?

My Belief Is Tied to My Identity and/or Out of My Control

In 2015, the publication of OKCupid founder Christian Rudder's book *Dataclysm: Love, Sex, Race, and Identity—What Our Online Lives Tell Us About Our Offline Selves*[2] revealed previously unknown data about the reality of online dating behavior. One of its most widely circulated revelations was related to Black women (followed by Asian men) being the least pursued demographic group on dating apps. Additionally, U.S. Census data reflects that Black women marry later in life and

---

2 Christian Rudder, *Dataclysm: Love, Sex, Race, and Identity—What Our Online Lives Tell Us About Our Offline Selves* (Crown, 2014).

less often than the general public.[3] These conclusions have continued to resonate with the experiences of many Black women online and in real life.

Taking this data at face value, it's no surprise that it has led to a belief many Black women hold—*I am a less desirable romantic partner.* As a Black woman, or anyone else holding a disempowering identity-based belief, you obviously can't change outside forces. Racism, sexism, ableism, homophobia, and more oppressive forces exist. I'm not suggesting otherwise. However, you must decide what you'll believe about your individual power to transcend them. There are people of your same identity who have true love relationships. Why not you?

Similarly, I've heard multiple women of all ages, but particularly above the age of 40, complain that men their age all want younger women. Let's say that's "true." Did love put an expiration date on you, or did society? If you think society is healthy and wise and makes decisions in our collective best interest, then following society's labels of you makes total sense. I promise you, if you want to see evidence of 40$^+$-year-old women falling in love and having incredible relationships, you can find it.

If I sound evangelical in my conviction that you can't both identify with and transcend unwanted outcomes, it's because I am. Perfect faith at every moment isn't required. Remember that we don't have to be perfect to have true love (we already have love's perfection within us), so don't worry about that. Simply recognize that if you believe in a universe where you personally have no ability to have the love you want due to *who* you are, it's going to be extremely difficult for you to manifest true love. Belief that love is the strongest force in the universe and that nothing excludes you from its power is worth adopting for yourself. It also happens to be true.

---

3 R. Kelly Raley, Megan M. Sweeney, and Danielle Wondra, "The Growing Racial and Ethnic Divide in U.S. Marriage Patterns," National Institutes of Health PubMed Central, https://pmc.ncbi.nlm.nih.gov/articles/PMC4850739/.

Straddling Conflicting Love Beliefs

Nate was dumbfounded. "All this time I thought she was the problem and I've been so angry at her. And now I realize I'm the asshole. I've been so mean to her!" My client had been at his wit's end with his girlfriend. Their relationship dynamic was like this: The more she leaned in, the more he leaned away. And when he occasionally leaned in, she stayed leaning in. Which freaked him out and caused him to push her away.

For over a year, their relationship had gone that way. One real sticking point for him was how quickly she bounced back from an argument once they had talked it out. Their communication, he admitted, was great. They'd talk about conflicts when they arose, which was fairly frequently because they both found themselves agitated often. After a heart-to-heart, his girlfriend would be ready to move on to the next topic of conversation. And it was driving him crazy. "I just don't understand how she can move on so quickly. It makes me feel like she's not taking it seriously enough." I asked him if he felt heard and resolved at the end of these talks. He said that he did. "In that case, would you rather she hang on to anger over a situation once you felt it had been resolved?" He laughed. "Oh damn. I never thought of the alternative. No, I would hate it if she did that!"

Nate came to realize he was in an inner tug-of-war between an old belief—*women make your life harder*—and the new belief he was now cultivating: *For me, the right partner enhances my life.* In his past relationships, this unwanted belief had played out in his pattern of falling hard, then freaking out and unconsciously causing strife in the relationship.

Breaking Unwanted Patterns

You have a beautiful mind. A complex psychology that contains more facets than even science can explain. You truly are amazing! You have a GENIUS subconscious mind that runs 95% of your life without you even knowing it. Pretty incredible, right?

If you have an unwanted relationship pattern, pause for a moment to appreciate the effectiveness of your subconscious genius. You are the common denominator in any pattern in your relationships. The same applies to any *wanted* pattern. Acknowledge your wanted life patterns and pause for a moment of gratitude. For instance, perhaps you're naturally attracted to high-integrity partners. Or you have a pattern of attracting loyal friends. The point is—patterns aren't inherently bad. They're how we maintain the status quo in our lives. When that status quo is wanted, great! But if and when you're ready for a transformation, that power is yours.

There is likely something in your current relationship pattern that works for you as well as something that doesn't. An example would be effortlessly meeting romantic prospects (wanted), but only being attracted to the ones who gaslight you (unwanted). The first step in breaking an unwanted pattern is to name it for what it truly is. Here are three critical questions that will help:

1. What is working in my relationship pattern? (In other words, what do I want more of?)
2. What isn't working in my relationship pattern? (In other words, what do I want to stop happening?)
3. What do I want my relationship pattern to be instead?

Another way of thinking of the preceding questions is, *What do I effortlessly attract, and what do I want to attract but can't seem to?* and *What would I love to attract instead?* Remember to ground yourself in compassionate curiosity as you reflect on these questions. If it takes time to reflect on them before you have an answer, that's perfectly normal. Clarity will come if that's what you're ready for.

Heartwork

Hopefully by now you're already beginning to chip away at any disempowering beliefs and the self-identity they foster. Complete this chapter's love beliefs exercise. Because it can be helpful to compare and contrast how belief operates in other areas, reflect on the following when it comes to not only love, but also your beliefs in general:

- Which of my beliefs serve me well? How and where do I see evidence of these beliefs at play in my life?
- Which of my patterns serve me well? How and where do I see evidence of these patterns at play in my life?
- Which beliefs/patterns have I already transformed for the better? How did I do that?

CHAPTER 7

listen to your inner wisdom

If not for the inner guidance system all life possesses, everything in the universe would be chaos. We can mathematically calculate how to land a spacecraft on a distant planet. That can only be done because the universe is not random. If it were, sometimes planets would orbit the sun, and other times not. Sometimes gravity would stop working on Earth, and humans would fly.

We're people, not planets, but we are hitching a ride through outer space on a big rock. We, too, have an inner guidance system. Multiple, actually. There's the physical level (you aren't making your heart beat, yet it does), and the emotional level tells us when something feels wonderful or awful. We use our inner mental processing to make decisions all the time. Your soul also has important information it's conveying to you at all times. (Much more on the soul's journey in chapter 9.)

The biggest mistake most people make is to focus solely on their thoughts, physical sensations of attraction, and their emotional reactions in relationships. In *The Big Leap*[1], author Gay Hendricks defines the "upper-limit problem" all of us possess to put an unconscious ceiling on how much happiness we can experience. If your "upper limit" is set to "miserable" then it will not feel good or comfortable or sustainable to feel "peaceful," and so peace will elude you. Self-awareness comes from knowing your own upper limits and remaining compassionate and honest about them as you expand past them. In the clarity of that space, you can know your truth. Your true inner wisdom transcends the upper-limit problem, so it really should have a bigger say in your romantic decision-making.

Happiness Is Good for Your Radar

The peace that joy brings will clear the static of anxiety, worry, and feelings of being disconnected from love. Peace is a higher form of consciousness, and from that place wisdom comes more easily. You already know that the calmer you are in a situation, the more clear you are about what needs to be done. This applies as much to your romantic journey as anything else.

"I'm in a good place right now. I don't need to be in a relationship" is a sentiment I've heard more times than I can count. As if being unhappy with your life *should* be the motivation for seeking a romantic partner (of course it often is). Being in a good place, or being happy single, is, in my opinion, the best place to be when co-creating a relationship with a romantic partner. Your relationship is just that—a co-creation of something brand-new that's never existed before. That relationship can't maintain any state of mutual joy unless you're both capable of being joyful.

---

1 Gay Hendricks, *The Big Leap: Conquer Your Hidden Fear and Take Life to the Next Level* (Harper One, 2010).

how to find true love

Know and Honor Yourself

The best investment you can ever make is to get to know yourself. There's no finish line where you have perfect insight into all parts of your psyche. Knowing oneself is an ongoing process, because to paraphrase the poet Walt Whitman, you really do contain multitudes. Different seasons of life bring new lessons to the surface. Honoring what that knowledge reveals is the secret sauce. It can be terrifying to listen to your inner truth, and following its guidance can be even scarier. Whether it's saying goodbye to a relationship or a job that no longer aligns with your purpose, or saying yes to an invitation to something new. I've observed a correlation between honoring your truth and getting what you want in relationships (and life) in my clients and my own life. It can be hard to know who you are when others are quick to tell you who you should be. Here are some tools that can help you discover how best to honor yourself in this season:

1. Journaling (can help you process your feelings and make sense of your experiences)
2. Working with a coach or therapist (for guidance, tools, and accountability)
3. Physical movement (to get out of your head and into your body, where feeling actually happens)
4. Seeking out new communities (for togetherness and support)
5. Dreaming up an "art project" for its own sake (to inspire and excite you)

I was stood up—in a restaurant, like a cringeworthy scene in a movie—on my 30th birthday. In that moment, when I realized the man I'd known for years, dated for months, and who'd texted me he was on his way an hour before wasn't coming? It turned out to be a moment of grace where I realized an invaluable lesson: *Listen to your intuition when something feels off about someone.* I'd talked myself into dating him, against my better judgment. And guess what? I never betrayed myself in that way ever again. If I'd not had that moment of clarity, who knows how many more inconsiderate people I would've rationalized dating. It wasn't the first time he'd showed me his selfishness, and yet I was still opening my heart to him in the name of being open and ready for love. He gave me a way better gift by standing me up than he would have by showing up. As far as these things can go, I got off easy and I take it as a win.

What You're Really Manifesting

Some people are uncomfortable with the word *manifestation*, but it's how life works. When there's anything my heart is being called to have, I take that as evidence that it's available to me, even if I don't know how it's going to happen. You might not label it as "manifesting," but you've probably had the same experience at various times in your life. Whether you're intentionally embracing manifestation as I do, or you're unconsciously manifesting, you're still playing a starring role in your life's consistent outcomes. Alice, my client who was stuck in an unwanted dating pattern, was powerfully manifesting what she did *not* want. She even had a mantra to support her efforts—"I'm going to be alone forever." Without clarity of your power and purpose, you can waste a lot of time and energy manifesting the wrong things.

When you set out to manifest (as in, make real in your life) a true love relationship, it's important to know what's in your control and what's not. I call this distinguishing between "your department" and "the universe's department." Your department isn't to imagine the perfect person and wait for them to materialize out of thin air or to control when they show up in your life. I've witnessed many people concentrate on a fully controlled view of their perfect person, with no success. That's because sometimes, as in the case of Harriet in chapter 2, that person doesn't exist, and even if they did, what she was focused on was unrelated to what their actual relationship would be.

Of course, you get to have your preferences. But releasing your attachment to them makes manifesting love easier. You don't have to worry—the universe isn't going to deliver you a soulmate you're not attracted to. Give yourself permission to welcome unexpected attractions. Particularly if you're focused on breaking a pattern—dating against type is worth exploring. What exactly your person "should" look like, what kind of job they have, and so on—that part you can't know. You might have a hunch, and maybe they'll truly be mostly as you expected. But perhaps not. Open up to allow yourself to be surprised in love. Otherwise, you will naturally play a scarcity game of "there are X number of people who meet Y criteria in my city." Don't ever forget that love is abundant. Single men who are 6'2" with blond hair, green eyes, and $100,000 in savings are not.

When you lose sight of the true nature of love, you might misunderstand your assignment, thinking it's your department to manifest someone within strict parameters, as Harriet did. Your department is to manifest the version of you that can recognize and receive the love you want. You do your assignment first, not the other way around. You're manifesting the skill at knowing how to recognize and receive a higher level of love. You're manifesting clarity and the know-how to make choices in alignment with the love you want. The courage to keep your heart open in spite of fear is your department. Everything outside of your control requires faith.

Shifting your love beliefs and breaking unwanted patterns, as you did in the previous chapter, is your department. As a reminder, you do not have to do anything in these pages or in life "perfectly" to have true love. Consider that the true love you want is available to you, and your department is to clear away any barriers to love as they arise.

Your Highest Good

Anything that moves you in the direction of more love is in your highest good. You have an inner compass (your soul), and you have the power to determine where it's pointing. Asking yourself the simple question "Is this in my highest good?" can reveal your next best steps toward self-love. If it doesn't honor you as your first and primary true love, it's not in your best interest. Believe it or not, if it's not in your highest good, it's not in anyone else's either. That means if your heart is telling you that you're in the wrong relationship, you are. Your partner might not agree, but listening to your inner wisdom is your job, not theirs. I've coached many clients through breakups and I've been through some painful ones myself. Everyone is on their own journey with their own lessons to learn. They, too, have an inner voice to discover and honor.

Following through on what you discover isn't always easy, but it is rewarding. For example, when you walk away from a relationship with someone who mistreats you, even when part of you can rationalize their actions, that is in your highest good. If you allow yourself to be vulnerable and honest with yourself about your feelings when it would be easier to ignore them, that's a self-loving action to take.

Navigating dating and relationships can be confusing and isolating. There's genuine pressure to prioritize external outcomes over the inner voice that's saying, "This doesn't feel right." Familial or peer group pressure is also a factor many have to work hard to overcome. I've heard stories from divorced clients who ignored the ringing of their inner alarm bells and got married anyway because they couldn't trust their gut and they didn't want to let others down.

We're not often aware of it, but we're all spiritually connected in this human family. Together we're collectively manifesting the world through how we show up in it. Sometimes what's in your highest good doesn't feel like it at the time. Being broken up with hurts, even when you know the relationship was toxic or unsustainable. When you're in the low emotions of heartbreak, it's not easy to see the larger journey at play. You deserve to be with someone who feels the same way as you and is ready to make the same commitment as you. It hurts, but ultimately them setting you free on your journey leads you closer to true love.

Listen to Your Heart

One of my clients relocated to a small city from a large one where she had a solid friend circle. Away from her community and working long hours in her new job, she'd devoted all of her mental energy and spare time to finding a boyfriend. Being part of a couple would provide built-in companionship to ease the loneliness she was feeling, she told me. When we began working together, she was almost two years into her quest and had gone on countless dates. But nothing was connecting. "I keep reaching the end of every dating app. I've already seen everyone single in this city."

As we talked more about her feelings of isolation in her new hometown, it became obvious she was placing the weight of outsized expectations on what her life would look like when she got into a relationship. What she really craved, in addition to a partner, was a community of friends who she could go out and do things with like she used to before her move. She didn't even want a boyfriend unless a community came as a package deal. "I'm only interested in dating people with existing friend circles I'd fit into," she told me.

I told her, "It sounds like what you need is your own friend circle," and I gave her heartwork around looking for activities where friend-making opportunities would flourish. Going to the movies alone? Something I personally love, but it's a solitary activity. But going to a film festival with panels and events? Much more social. And that's exactly where she made a friend who eventually introduced her to more people in the community.

"I went bowling with some random guys I just met through this new acquaintance and flirted with one of them all night. I'd forgotten flirting could be fun!" she reported after her first date with random bowling guy, who became her boyfriend soon thereafter. "I was definitely more attractive and confident being silly in a bowling alley with a guy I had no investment in than on a Hinge date. I didn't expect to see him again, so I just had fun with it."

By following what her heart was craving—not just romance, but community too—she got both. I've witnessed this phenomenon many times when people start doing the things they're being called to. When you understand that your romantic relationship doesn't exist to be your everything, you start living more fully.

Trusting Yourself

Because our inner lives can get anxious, chaotic, and otherwise fraught, you might have difficulty trusting yourself. Past relationship choices, particularly if they resulted in trauma and/or are symptomatic of a larger pattern, can cause you to doubt your inner voice. Because we live in a society that doesn't generally value inner wisdom, you might be out of touch or practice with hearing yours. As a child, you might have been shamed out of following your own guidance. None of these are insurmountable obstacles to strengthening your intuitive muscles. Go slow and steady as you proceed in romance, paying attention to the whispers and nudges that arise. Practice being present and aware of your feelings, thoughts, and physiology. If your heart and thoughts are racing, prioritize grounding yourself to a calmer state. Your old patterns need the distraction of static to keep running without you noticing what's going on. Breathwork, movement, and any practice that grounds you in the present (such as meditation) will help clear that static. From this state, you can and will make better decisions.

What You Focus on Expands

The simplest distinction between people who struggle with dating and those who don't is what they focus on. The more outwardly focused you are in dating, the more disempowered you are when it comes to long-term relationship skill building.

My mentor, author Paul C. Brunson, has a saying: "The best time to work on your marriage is before you get married." I'll take that one step further—the best time to work on your future relationship is before you're in it. Dating is a process I'm so passionate about because, as I've said, dating skills are love skills. Nothing you've experienced romantically is meaningless; learn the lessons and move on to the next phase, or you're doomed to repeat this one. For example, discerning what compatibility looks like for you is a skill that makes dating easier and ensures you're picking people you can grow together with over time.

When people are more focused on the things you can observe at a glance or on paper, they have more difficulty. I'm not saying that never yields a successful relationship. For some, buying a lottery ticket is the path to lasting wealth. But even in that dream scenario, for most who win, their riches are short-lived.

Windfalls of love, just like windfalls of money, happen every day. I'm willing to bet they've happened to you, even if you didn't recognize what was happening. The 50 percent of lottery winners who go bankrupt after achieving their dream of getting rich didn't understand what it took to keep their money, to grow their money, and to achieve the lasting wealth they truly wanted. They got rich, but how they "did" money didn't level up with their bank account. Love works the same way. If love feels absent from your life and you're waiting on an outside person to give it to you, it'll be harder to hold on to it when that person does show up.

If you want someone to see the real you—the unshakeable you that's always been and always will be in there—it's time to focus on your own capacity for that level of vulnerability. "Isn't love supposed to be easy? Shouldn't it just happen?" one of my clients pleaded with me. The true answer is no. Love is not passive—passive love is neglectful, which is inherently unloving. You can waste your energy wishing that growing into a life full of love was effortless, or you can accept that effort is required. Then you can get to work—not like a job that you're doing for someone else, but like an assignment for your soul. An assignment no one grades and you have endless chances to complete, but an assignment nonetheless.

Finding True Meaning in Where You've Been

There are countless examples of people telling me a story that goes something like this:

"Person treats me terribly and I hate it. We fight. We make up. They keep treating me terribly and I'm so frustrated. I am doing so much for them. We keep fighting and they keep doing the same thing. They are making me miserable. Why won't they stop treating me so terribly? Why can't they just love me and let us be happy? I've done so much for them and I even sacrificed something important for them. They never repay me! What can I do to make them love me? I just don't understand why they keep doing this. What did I do to deserve this? They are so terrible."

It's easy to point the finger of blame at someone who treats you badly or triggers an old wound. It goes without saying that you deserve better; the more salient question is why are you settling for so little? The simplest answer to that question is some part of you didn't feel safe consistently receiving love. That's the part that chose to put up with that relationship dynamic. So while it doesn't feel good to be treated poorly, it might feel *familiar*. If it's all you've ever known in relationships, you must show yourself love with the same level of devotion you're seeking from someone else.

Much of this book focuses on your inner world, because that is where you must normalize true love in order to make it inevitable on the outside. Aligning yourself with the energy of love doesn't require perfection—only intention. You have the power to send love to that part of yourself who rationalizes unloving treatment and to move forward in spite of that inner misunderstanding. That's taking high-self-worth action—your feelings are not required, only your commitment to love.

Nourishing Your Non-romantic Relationships

TFIC places romantic love on a towering pedestal as the highest form of love. When you abandon love hierarchies and choose instead to center love in your life, you see the importance of holistically celebrating love. Friendships, family, and communities of all kinds are valuable to your overall happiness and feelings of connectedness. The U.S. Surgeon General didn't recommend dating as the cure to the loneliness and isolation epidemic. Instead, he recommended human connection through community, friendship, and platonic relationships. The cure for the mental health crisis is to come together, as we've done as humans for far longer than we've had social media.

In the digital era, your intention is required to nourish your relationships beyond a screen. Having tons of social media followers is an insufficient substitute for sitting across the table from a live human who cares about you. Don't overburden your romantic partners by expecting them to do the work of a whole network of people that humans have relied on for millennia. We used to gather in religious institutions, town squares, civic organizations, and tribes. Times have changed, but our need for each other hasn't. Connection is what allows us to thrive as humans.

On that front, it's a common occurrence that some people ghost their friends once they find a romantic partner. I understand the temptation to break away and isolate together, but studies show that relationship satisfaction is positively associated with having social connections in addition to your partner. May I suggest allowing for friendship and romance? For community and coupledom? Let your focus be a both/and, not an either/or.

Heartwork

Reflect on the following:

1. How invested are you in your own happiness? Do you take responsibility for it, or do you look to outside people or events to bring happiness to you?
2. How well do you know yourself? Is your relationship with you a priority?
3. When has your inner knowing been so strong you couldn't ignore it? Did you listen or did you override it with thinking? What happened next?
4. What does becoming a more loving version of you look and feel like? Would you be more forgiving, less judgmental, have better boundaries to protect yourself from harm, etc.?
5. Do you feel connected to your inner wisdom and have confidence you can make decisions in your highest good? How can you cultivate more confidence in this area?
6. Have you undervalued or taken your non-romantic relationships for granted? How might you begin to invest more of yourself in all the important relationships in your life?

7. On your love journey, in what way(s) have you been focused on the "lack" or absence of romantic love? In what way(s) have you been focused on cultivating and appreciating love independent of your relationship status?

CHAPTER 8

balance your head and your heart

Decisions, decisions...Early dating can be nerve-racking when it doesn't work out, and maybe even more so when it does. By "work out" I mean you've met someone you like, they like you, and things are progressing—you're spending time together, you're learning about each other's lives, and you're hot for each other. It's what you want as the precursor to your ultimate manifestation, a true love partnership. As intoxicating as it can be to fall for someone new, it can also be fraught with anxiety and worry about making the wrong choice or not being "chosen" by your new boo.

"When you know, you know." "I can tell right away if they're for me or not." These are sentiments I often hear from people who have consistently chosen toxic partners. What you and everyone "know" on the level of energetic attraction is who is a match for your love program. The beliefs, identities, expectations about love that we've been discussing? They all make up your love program. In romance, certainty is what so many are seeking. But they fail to recognize this basic fact—who you are attracted to is not random, nor is it as superficial as it might appear. In my experience, many people overestimate their ability to determine quickly whether someone is a good match. (This is especially true on dating apps.) The quest for certainty, when extreme, becomes its own love block. You can watch an episode or two of *Love Is Blind* or *The Bachelorette* to see these certainty blinders play out across multiple dysfunctional relationship dynamics.

In this chapter, we turn our attention to compatibility and how to use both your head and your heart to discern what kind of relationship will bring you the lasting love you desire. It is a blessing to have the chance to get clear on that before you get into a relationship. By knowing what's right for you before you commit to another person, you save yourself the frustration of trying to make the unworkable work.

Success in love (and life) requires a balancing of your head and your heart. With the right love-centered mindset, your head can provide you the emotional safety you need to give and receive love. That's why so much of this book is about your thoughts and beliefs, because that's your starting point in relationships. Emotional safety isn't required only for a healthy romantic partnership; it's also required for a healthy relationship with yourself.

Stay in Love Forever

Drs. John Gottman and Julie Schwartz Gottman are a married couple who've been researching relationships, counseling married couples, and writing books about making love last for decades. They speak to a fundamental truth in their book *Eight Dates: Essential Conversations for a Lifetime of Love*[1] when they write "[a] true love story isn't a fairy tale. It takes vulnerability and effort. The reward is that you love your

---

1   John Gottman, Julie Schwartz Gottman, Doug Abrams, and Rachel Carlton Abrams, *Eight Dates: Essential Conversations for a Lifetime of Love* (Workman, 2019).

partner more on your fiftieth anniversary than you did on your wedding night. You can stay in love forever."

I think of staying in love forever as choosing to treat each other with love forever. And to do that, we have to hone our skill at sustaining love. With the commitment to your increased love skills, the emotion of being in love flows naturally. It's easy to fall in love when someone you adore is showering you with acts of love and devotion. But when life is life-ing, and disagreement arises as it inevitably will, the commitment to love must be strong and consistent for the feelings of being in love to continue. With self-compassionate curiosity, can you genuinely say you've made that commitment to anyone in the past, starting with yourself? Have you chosen people in the past who were skilled at love? Have you been?

Choose a Higher-Level Relationship

Have you ever been on a date with someone you wanted to like, but being around them bummed you out too much? Or been turned off by someone's constant anger or defensiveness? How about noticing their rude behavior toward you or others? For many of my clients, when casual relationships with indifferent partners lose their appeal, that's their signal to get serious about calling in more. So if you're turned off by the thought of being in a toxic relationship, congratulations! That means you're ready for an advanced level, one based more in love than fear. Despite many opinions to the contrary, simply being in a relationship is not the prize. You are the prize, and you deserve to have the highest level love your heart and soul are calling you to experience.

The higher/lower designation might come across as judgmental, which isn't my intention. However, you can look at life and see that your view of an ideal relationship has advanced since adolescence. As you mature and evolve, so do your relationships. Your past likely contains some relationship dynamics you'd never dream of tolerating now. That's what you advancing to a higher level looks like. The more love that's actively embodied in your relationship, the higher the level, which also means the greater the capacity for love required. Relationships dominated by abuse, resentment, fear, or dishonesty are lower level, even when the partners *feel* love for each other. Some people who love you aren't capable of loving you at the level of true love. It's not because they don't feel it; it's because they don't know how to consistently *do* love.

A higher, or more advanced level relationship is always possible, whether people realize it or not. Accessing it requires a level of intentionality and personal responsibility that you already have—otherwise you wouldn't have been drawn to this book. Needless to say, many of our human family don't (yet) possess this understanding of love. On your dating journey, you *will* encounter people more committed to lower-level relationships than you are. Some of them will pursue you, some will succumb to you, and some might be soulmates but not lifelong partners. Expect to learn the lessons each "level" has to show you. If you choose your partners mindfully and with love, you will advance to higher (and deeper) levels of love together.

Unconditional Love

Does unconditional love exist? My strong belief is yes, it does. However, if you equate unconditional love with unconditionally *feeling* love, then no, it doesn't. Expecting to always feel loving toward anyone, regardless of what they say or do, isn't what I mean by unconditional love. There are saints among us who can do that, and hopefully that's where humanity is headed for all. But for now, for most of us, unconditional love must be a choice in how we treat ourselves and others. The verb *to love* is ours to claim.

Tap into Your Love Vision

Clarity on what you don't want in a partnership is critical in discerning what you do want. Get in tune with what your heart wants beyond the conditioning of your mind. What do you most want to experience with your partner? How will you feel when you are together? If no one else was going to see your partner or know their résumé, what would bring you the most fulfillment in your relationship? It's important to move beyond the "list" of dream partner traits (height, body type, job, hobbies, net worth) to the relationship you'll build together.

Instead of just writing a list, writing down your love vision is a powerful way to tap into the energy and emotion of the relationship you're already calling in. I encourage you to take some time to reflect on and craft your vision. It doesn't have to be more than a few lines, and it only has to resonate with you on a level beyond the superficial. Here are some questions to assist you in bringing your vision forward:

1. What would I love to feel while being intimate (emotionally and physically) with my partner?
2. How would I love us to communicate with each other?
3. What dynamic(s) would I love to share in our relationship?
4. What would make me feel completely safe and unconditionally loved? How do I want to express unconditional love and safety?
5. What do I most dream of sharing with my partner in our time together?

Sample answers:

1. Cherished and seen.
2. With unconditional respect and honesty.

3. I want us to both know we have each other's backs and we're always rooting for each other.
4. I'd feel loved by being treated kindly and I'd feel safe if I knew we wouldn't intentionally try to hurt each other.
5. I want us to have a family that we're equally invested in and prioritize.

Sample answers rewritten as a first-person love vision:

1. I feel cherished and seen while we're being intimate.
2. We communicate respectfully and honestly, even when we disagree.
3. We're each other's biggest cheerleaders and supporters.
4. We express our love for each other by treating each other kindly and never being intentionally hurtful, so we both feel safe to be our authentic selves.
5. We share a love of family and building a life together with a family of our own.

Turning your answers into first-person, present-tense statements can function as the start of your love vision. Experiment with it and tweak it until it resonates within you. Listen to your heart to determine what level of relationship you're being called to have. Once it feels good and aligned with your heart, read it daily or whenever you want a love boost.

Escape the "Projection Field"

The definition of *projection* is "imagining that someone else feels a particular emotion or wants something when in fact it is you who feels that way." The fairy-tale mindset encourages this in our relationships, as does dating culture. Psychiatrist Christine B. L. Adams describes a common phenomenon in the early phases of relationships this way: "[o]ne person may hold a high standard and opinion of the other, unwarranted by who that person is and how they behave and think."[2]

The modern approach to dating is often rooted in projection. The "projection field" is what I call the mental space of dating based on preconceived or imagined notions. With this approach, you overestimate your ability to determine compatibility based on who you think the other person is instead of seeing them truthfully. Assumptions about compatibility are a form of projection. We assume that because we are one way, those we're interested in are the same. A simple example is "They know I want a committed relationship, so if they're dating me, they must want that too." Conflating certain traits with character is another sneaky form of projection. "They must be successful because they drive an expensive car" is an assumption. Perhaps you wouldn't buy a luxury car unless you could comfortably afford it, but that doesn't mean someone else shares your approach to financial decisions. Countless times, disappointed clients have vented their frustration about someone's behavior, or what they learn when they start having real conversations about values. When we project negative traits on someone else, based on assumptions, we can also miss out. I once had a client who'd assumed that since a person he'd been set up with on a blind date was a yoga teacher, she wasn't ambitious or the "kind of professional" he'd be compatible with. As it turned out, she owned her own successful studio, had high-profile private clients, and was in the process of writing a book.

Like a projection on a movie screen, it's easy to convince yourself a romantic projection is real, and you can imagine your love interests to be whoever you want. If you're not careful, you can mistake your partner for someone with different motivations and qualities than they truly

---

2   Christine B. L. Adams, "How to Deal with Projections in Relationships," *Psychology Today*, February 2, 2024, https://www.psychologytoday.com/us/blog/living-on-automatic/202402/how-to-deal-with-projections-in-relationships.

possess. By recognizing this potential pitfall, you empower yourself to transcend it and discover the reality of who another person truly is.

Chosen vs. Choosing Each Other

Maya and I began working together shortly after she'd rekindled a romance with someone she'd casually hooked up with in the past. "I really need your help so I don't f*ck this up," she told me in our first session.

So I asked, "What specifically are you concerned about? What does 'f*ck this up' mean?"

She went on to explain how in the past, she had a habit of picking fights and holding grudges that pushed partners away.

"Let's take a step back," I suggested. "When you're with someone you like—on a date, or just spending time together, how do you feel? How do you feel with this guy?" Maya was unsure. "I don't know how to answer that. I feel…nervous? Anxious." Next, I asked her what she liked about him. She began to list some of his traits, like his ambition, how well-traveled he was, how funny and smart and good-looking he was.

Our conversation continued as I asked Maya more questions designed to get her to articulate what she felt for him beyond liking some of these easily observable, "on paper" characteristics. She was at a loss. "I just like that he's putting in the effort to spend time with me, and the last time we were hooking up, he didn't do that. But I don't know how I feel with him that's any different than how I feel when I'm interested in anyone. Just nervous I'm going to f*ck it up, I guess!"

Maya's situation is an extremely common one. She was so fearful that she'd do something "wrong" in this budding romance that she wasn't able to be present and aware of whether she actually enjoyed his company. In other words, she was more focused on him "choosing" her than she was on even determining whether she wanted to choose him back. Luckily, they had a date scheduled the following night and I was able to give her immediate heartwork to be present with her feelings on the date. Maya needed to get out of her head and into her body—that's where we *feel* our feelings. Overthinking, anxiety, and shame cloud much judgment in life and certainly in dating. Together, she and I made a plan for her to be present on her date, which included some pre-date intention-setting and deep breathing to calm her anxious thoughts. I challenged her to focus on her breath throughout the night and let herself *feel* instead of thinking nonstop.

The next day, I received this text message from Maya:

The date went really well. I took your advice to focus on how I was feeling, which really did help me stay present. It felt good! Thank you for the guidance—it's already helping!

Over the next few weeks, Maya was able to get clarity on what she liked about *being with* him, not just *about* him in the abstract.

You're not Cinderella—simply being chosen from the crowd isn't the goal if true love is what you seek. Reciprocal enthusiasm and appreciation for each other is what elevates a relationship from the transactional act of "checking boxes" to the genuine connection your heart truly craves.

Raise Your Standards

When people learn I'm a love coach, I often hear an unprompted, defensive version of "Well, I've waited this long and I'm not going to settle. If you know where I can find someone who meets my standards, I'm all ears." I usually explain to them that standards should be viewed as the quality of the relationship, not the traits possessed by your partner. Being with someone who looks like a dream but treats you like a nightmare (or even just an afterthought) is having low standards. Often those with the strictest "standards" about who they date are the same ones with the lowest standards in terms of how they're treated by those same people. If you are willing to settle for poor treatment in dating, much less an unfulfilling relationship for the long haul, you are settling. How sexy, smart, or high status your partner is won't and doesn't change that.

Committing to prioritizing how you're treated in relationships above all else is an act of self-love. Which doesn't mean you don't get to have preferences in who you date, of course. It simply means that preferences don't override the reality of what it will feel like to be in a relationship with that person. Raise your standards to the high level dynamic of true love, and transform your dating life. As a refresher, a true love relationship has a foundation of the following:

- Unconditional love (in action)
- Unconditional respect
- Emotional intimacy
- Physical intimacy
- Emotional safety
- Physical safety
- Commitment
- Adoration
- Joy

For example, if you only emotionally invest in people who treat you with unconditional respect, you will naturally have higher quality relationships than if you tolerate disrespect. If you only commit to people with a demonstrated capacity and willingness to reciprocate, you'll have more emotional safety in your relationships as a result. It's not always easy to believe those people are out there, but I promise you they exist. You can only become a match for them by saying no to those who can't or won't show up for you with the treatment you deserve.

Relationship Values = Relationship Needs

I love the way author and professor Adam Grant, in several interviews, defines *values*: "Beliefs are what we think is true. Values are what we think is important." In life and in love, we have to prioritize what's most important in the countless decisions required day in and day out. We're always making choices, but how often do they align with what we really think is important? In romance, TFIC has its own definitions of value. Only you can decide for yourself what's most important to you.

Earlier in this chapter you started crafting your love vision. As you move forward, keep it in mind as you're dating and deciding who to emotionally invest in. If you meet someone who's really amazing, but they don't share any of your values around the actual relationship you'd build, what kind of life will you have together?

The seductive dating trap is: *I can convince this person to want what I want.* Or *I can ignore the disconnect and keep going. After all, they're the kind of person I want to be with.* No matter how many boxes someone checks on your list, you're not setting yourself up to win in love if you dishonor your own values.

Needs-First Dating vs. Wants-First Dating

Naturally, you must meet a human in the world to be your true love partner. At this point in your life, you probably know a lot about what you're attracted to romantically and sexually. The people who embody those traits can easily become your mental blueprint for compatibility. For instance, I have a friend who won't consider dating anyone who isn't her physical ideal. Her commitment to this ideal leads her to tolerating a lot of mismatches in terms of character, relationship goals, values, and even how she's treated, as long as they meet her surface criteria. This is "wants-first" dating—when you prioritize your superficial preferences over the relationship itself. It's a bit like always eating cake when you're hungry instead of a nourishing meal.

Wants-first dating fosters a scarcity mindset about love. If you're only open to considering people who meet your surface criteria, then you'll be limited in love by what you can observe on the outside. This is a big part of why people fail at dating apps—the technology encourages you to date on a surface level. It's easy to filter yourself into a tiny subset of daters based on qualities you can assess by which boxes have been checked on their profile. Dating apps provide the perfect tools for superficial pickiness and snap judgments based on perceived attractiveness. If you've ever been disappointed (or pleasantly surprised) by someone's appearance in real life versus their online photos, you know firsthand how big the gap between virtual perception and reality can be. And yet, many people continue with the same ineffective strategy of valuing that perception over the reality underneath.

By contrast, "needs-first" dating means that your priority is the relationship itself. It looks like valuing your need for safety and intimacy as non-negotiables, not "on paper" characteristics. Needs-first dating doesn't mean none of your preferences matter—we all need some cake! But if you value your preferences as much as or more than your needs, that's a sneaky way of settling for a relationship that doesn't fulfill you. Needs-first dating requires examining and prioritizing the things that have the most impact on your actual relationship.

It takes a higher level of intention to focus on quality over appearances. *How well do we get along? Are we on the same page about our love goals? Do I feel safe with this person? Are we able to see each other for who we are beyond the superficial?* These are questions you can only answer by being an active participant in choosing a partner and building a lasting partnership together. Looks and circumstances change over time. But can you co-create chemistry in sustainable ways that aren't dependent on abs, eye color, or how much money they make? These are the kinds of reflections that take more time and effort to discern than your wants. And this kind of relationship takes more skill to build than the fairy-tale version of love. Future you will thank you for your investment.

Identifying Your Core Romantic Values

If your true love relationship is a house, the true love values are the foundation and your romantic values are the bones of the house—its very structure. What happens in those rooms is your life within that relationship. In other words, the day-to-day reality of being in a relationship with someone doesn't just happen randomly. You use the kitchen in the house you built, even if you'd prefer a different design. In your relationship, you communicate in a way you've jointly established, even if it's ineffective. It's not so easy to make structural changes to a house or to long-established dynamics between partners.

The gift of being single and aware in this day and age is the ability to decide now, before you've committed to a long-term partnership, what a solid foundation and strong structure look and feel like for you. Imagine I have a magic wand, and with it I can materialize a person who possesses every dream characteristic you can imagine. They check every box on the list, and they come programmed to want to be with you. Now what? You've got the perfect-looking house with maximum curb appeal. Still, you wouldn't be indifferent to what's on the inside. You will care about what it's like to live in this house, no matter how lovely it looks from afar. Your happiness will differ depending on if it's warm and welcoming or a house of horrors.

The feeling you want inside your relationship is pointing you to your heart-centered romantic needs. It might be different, at least partly, from what you've prioritized in the past. For example, because I've worked with mostly high-achieving professionals, I've often had clients tell me they need a partner with a college or an advanced degree. I'm not knocking higher education (I have a law degree), but a degree just hangs on the wall. What do you really want? What is the relationship between that degree and what it's like to live in that house? What is the relationship between the degree and what's inside that person?

In response to these types of questions, the truth usually comes out when they start to express the "why" of this requirement. Count-less times I've heard a version of "If they have a degree, then they won't be intimidated by mine and we'll be intellectually matched." What I hear in these explanations is the underlying, true needs being expressed—to have a partner who supports and roots for your success and to be intellectually stimulated. If you see yourself in a relationship with a dynamic of support and mental connection, amazing! Now you've identified two core relationship needs.

My invitation to you is to identify your top five core romantic values. In my experience, most people are surprised by how simple their needs are when they get down to it. You've been conditioned to think your partner has to be everything and more and don't forget rich and the best lover you've ever had and also your best friend and of course, perfect. You've been told you also have to be perfect to be good enough to be loved. But the heart and soul aren't seeking perfection in order to love and be loved. On the deepest level, you're seeking the safety of alignment.

Common Romantic Values

What is the metaphorical house you want to build together? What does it feel like to live inside? How do you interact? What do you prioritize between you? Here are some examples of common romantic values:

- Abundant living
- Acceptance
- Adventure
- Caretaking
- Deep emotional sharing
- Empathy
- Exploration and travel
- Faith/religious devotion
- Family
- Fitness
- Friendship
- Fun and playfulness
- Healthy living

- Intellectual stimulation
- Interdependence
- Optimism
- Personal growth
- Protectiveness
- Reassurance/support
- Reciprocity
- Service to community/family

- Sexual exploration and adventure
- Sexual intimacy
- Spiritual growth
- Support and encouragement
- Trust
- Vulnerability
- Wealth building

Feel free to add your own!

Heartwork

Complete the Aligned Values exercise at www.francescahogi.com/resources. Once you have your top five romantic values, reflect on the following:

1. How well am I embodying these values now?
2. In the past, have I chosen people who embodied these values? How was our relationship impacted?
3. In the past, have I prioritized my needs or my wants in dating? How will I balance the two going forward?
4. What step(s) can I commit to in order to center my romantic values now?

STEP 3

connect with a higher love (soulset)

CHAPTER 9

align with the energy of romantic flow

So far we've focused on bringing your attention to how you think and feel about yourself when it comes to love. Now we're turning to the role of your spirit, or soul, in your love journey. Love is spiritual, and when you honor it as such, you increase your connection to it. A simple and logical definition of spirituality I like is "the quality of being concerned with the human spirit or soul as opposed to material or physical things."

When you tune into yourself, beyond your thoughts and physical body, even beyond your emotions, which always fluctuate, you can probably sense a deep calling to love. You can change your mind or your behavior, but that calling doesn't go away, does it? That's why the absence of deep love is so painful. The call to love is a calling of your soul. The whole concept of soulmates is that you and another person recognize and feel a pull to each other on a level beyond the mind. In dating, we often treat the soul's calling as incidental, or something that will be satisfied by simply "being in a relationship." If you've had enough disappointing relationship experiences, you might become disillusioned in love because that call is not being answered, and it can be hard to know what to do about it.

There's another way. In this section, I hope to show you what's really going on here and how to practically answer this call to love.

The Soul

Is there a more existential question than the nature of the soul? I don't claim to possess the answers to all the mysteries of existence. However, what resonates for me is that the soul, the you underneath your personality and appearance, is connected to life force, or spiritual energy. Your soul is steady in its orientation toward love. It is beyond the power of human ego and dysfunction to corrupt or distort. A helpful analogy for the soul is that of a compass. You might be lost in the woods, but your compass is always pointing due north. You can spend as much time as you need taking detours or pulling off to the side of the road, but your soul never wavers. It's ever unfolding and evolving along with you, always pointing to a higher love.

Energy

Spiritual energy is the life force that animates every living thing in the universe, including you. In Sanskrit, it's called *prana*. Chinese philosophers named it *Chi*. Some people call it *God, spirit, joie de vivre*, or *love*. Science provides a correlation on the physical plane in atoms, the building blocks of matter. Your spiritual energy can't be seen by a specialized microscope like an atom can, but that doesn't make it any less real. As a living being in this universe, you are a manifestation of life force on an energetic level in both scientific and spiritual terms.

Your essence is felt and expressed in your energy at any given time. You know that when you feel good, you're thinking positively or feeling inspired; other people receive you differently than when you're angry or depressed, even when you attempt to hide those emotions. The ability to perceive other people's energy is evident when you meet certain people. At times, you get a vibe so strong it grabs your attention. Sometimes it's magnetic, like physical chemistry, or instant friendship, and other times it's repelling, like when someone gives you "the creeps." You might not always notice it consciously, but you're always sensing everything. Your energy is always traveling with you, reflecting your inner world out and filtering the outside world in through its perceptive power.

As we covered in chapter 6, everyone has a relationship pattern, though they can and do change. It's helpful to understand attraction intellectually, because your mind is a beautiful aspect of you, but that's not where the conversation ends. The way we unconsciously play out our relationship patterns is through attraction and repulsion, and that is purely energetic. We are attracted to the same dynamics in people, before we even realize those dynamics are present, because our energy is sensing something in their frequency that matches ours on that level.

Because it is so easy to convince ourselves that our attractions are inevitable and out of our control, it is easy to overlook this essential aspect of your romantic life. You are aligned with certain energies on the frequency of romance (as well as friendship, money, etc.), and that default alignment will dictate your love life unless and until you align yourself with a higher vision of the love you want.

Romantic Energy

The scientific definition of energy is "the capacity to do work." You have capacity, or energy, for different aspects of life. There's mental energy, which can be depleted after a long day of work or intense concentration. Your creative energy might ebb and flow depending on how inspired you feel at any given time. Energy isn't static, and neither is your access to different energetic frequencies within you. Romantic flow, like all spiritual aspects of being, can be blocked and also cleared. Your ease with attracting different dynamics, experiences, and opportunities is connected to how strong your energy is at various frequencies. Romantic energy is no exception.

Some people are magnets for romantic encounters, and others are cut off from their mojo entirely. In the fairy-tale version of love, your romantic energy is awakened when you meet The One, like in *Sleeping Beauty* or *How Stella Got Her Groove Back*. It certainly can and does occasionally happen that someone you encounter has just the right energetic cocktail within them to activate you from the outside in. However, I don't recommend relying on an outside jump start when you can do it yourself. One of my favorite classes to teach is called Romantic Activation, a two-month deep dive into giving dormant romantic energy a much-needed jolt.

Watching my students blossom into more excitement, open-heartedness, and love confidence is extremely gratifying. At the start of the course, one student, Dylan, didn't see themselves as romantically attractive. Growing up queer, they didn't have the same comfort with dating and receiving romantic attention as many of their straight peers, and they thought "hot" people were out of their league. Dylan had one of the fastest and most dramatic energetic shifts I've ever witnessed. They bravely leaned into all class heartwork, from practicing flirting to challenging their previous limited view of themselves. By the end of two months, Dylan was a straight-up vixen, flirting up a storm and finally going after the people they wanted, instead of settling for who they assumed would be into them. Shortly after the course, Dylan started dating someone who was "hot" (and many other great things) and years later, they're still happily together.

How to unblock your romantic frequency:

1. Set an intention to discover, or rediscover, your inner mojo.
2. Push yourself out of your comfort zone by practicing flirting (see chapter 13 for much more on this topic).
3. Observe what's blocking you from accessing the more romantic part of yourself—is it a lack of self-care or negative self-talk? You can release any block by first identifying it and challenging its validity.
4. Discover what makes you feel attractive or sexy. Commit to tangible steps to access that energy more often.
5. Identify where you're holding back in terms of vulnerability, connecting with others, and being seen. What's the story, or explanation underneath your hesitation? Revisit the romantic identity and belief exercises in chapter 6 to challenge any disempowering narratives about yourself.

Split Energy

Your thoughts influence your energy, and your energy influences your thoughts. It can seem that your mind is in the driver's seat of your life. But that doesn't account for why it's common to be attracted to the opposite of what you want. You might want to save money, eat better, or choose emotionally available partners. And yet, wanting and thinking alone doesn't make it so. When you have a disconnect between what you want and what you experience romantically (or otherwise), your energy is being split into more than one direction, disrupting flow. Like misaligned tires on a car, your conflicting energies might be leading you in opposing directions.

Let's look at the very common disconnect of wanting true love while simultaneously only being attracted to unavailable people.

That's your energy, unconsciously guiding you and your energetic match to each other. It's the subconscious genius that keeps our patterns' status quo. If you are only available in your mind, thinking, *I want true love* but your heart is saying *I must be perfect to be loved*, your energy will be split between these conflicting messages. We are not the logical beings we like to think we are. There's much more going on than what we've been taught to pay attention to.

Feelings of being not good enough are an emotional manifestation of a painful underlying love belief. On the energetic level, that belief manifests as attractions to people who have their own false love beliefs to contend with. It's the same energy split that draws you together, and might eventually tear you apart. Because it feels like we're victims of these people (and some may indeed have been abusers), it's often hard to see the deeper love lesson their presence in your life signals.

All of which is to say, when we learn our love lessons, we become more available. If you or someone you know has ever broken a toxic dating cycle, you can see how each relationship going forward is a higher level than ever before. They learned something new about themselves and what they deserve because of what they went through. The attraction that had trapped them in a toxic cycle is forever broken as their energy becomes more consistently aligned with what they actually want. You know you've expanded on an energetic level when your attractions change. Once you struggle to remember how and why you were ever so attracted to dysfunction in the first place, you know you've *really* moved on.

Every one of us has the power to align with the energy of our soul's deepest desires. Your attractions shift when your energy aligns. By committing to this journey, you've already begun shifting your energy. In this process, it's helpful to decide if you're ready to learn from love or from pain. Ever dated someone despite knowing it was going to end badly? Confessed your undying love for someone who's never shown the slightest romantic interest in you? That part of us is choosing to learn from pain.

Pain teaches, but so does love. You don't have to be starved of oxygen to love it; you can take a long, deep breath in gratitude for your life. Rooted in a foundation of self-love, you have everything you need to learn from love. Without being aware of the role energy plays in your attractions, you risk unconsciously stepping into an unwanted loop. Curiosity is love. Self-reflection (without judgment) is love. Give yourself permission to bring understanding to your romantic energy so you can change it if it no longer serves you.

Relationship Dynamics

Relationships each have their own dynamics, or energy. In chapter 8, I asked you to mentally decide which dynamics you most want to experience in your true love partnership. In this chapter, I'm challenging you to go beyond the mind and to a place of energetic knowing. It can be easy to dismiss the unwanted parts of your past relationships (especially the ones where you were hurt) as being your ex's fault.

However, what happens in any of our relationships doesn't exist in a vacuum. All of your relationships—romantic, familial, platonic, professional, etc., are distinct. They feel different in ways you can intellectualize, but only *know* by the experience of being in them. If you have more than one sibling, or friend, or colleague, you can easily observe that the dynamics in your relationships with them differ. You don't have the exact same relationship with any two people, as each person is unique.

Romantic relationships are a place where we can observe how our most consistent dynamics play out. Nothing is your "fault"—but it is your responsibility to face if you want better relationships in the future. You are half of the equation, always. When you shift your focus in dating from it being all about the other person to what you actually co-create together, it becomes much easier to intuitively feel who is and who isn't the right match for you.

Being in Your Own Energy

When you are still, when you are quiet and undistracted, you will come to know your own energy. Small children are good at modeling this for us. Have you ever observed a child happily in their own energetic bubble? Without self-consciousness or worry? Doing their thing without a care in the world? It's a beautiful, even enviable state of being to witness. They have the benefit of not yet being conditioned to think distracting thoughts about what they should do, how they should be, or what is expected of them. They simply are themselves.

Thinking, especially when thoughts become unproductive either due to negativity or rumination, can take you far from your own natural energetic state. But while your thoughts can be a huge distraction, they are an indication of what's standing between you and your true energy. How you "feel" goes beyond your emotions. We tend to label emotions in the mind, such as *I'm sad* or *angry* or *happy*. Your energy is more subtle, and the more disconnected we are from our physical being and the present moment, the harder it will be to know our own energy.

Growing more comfortable with your thoughts, feelings, and energy helps you to:

- identify where you're out of alignment with your soul's calling;
- normalize feeling good on your own;
- normalize being still and minimizing distraction;
- normalize trusting yourself on a soul level;
- recognize when other people are positively or negatively impacting you by their presence and actions;

- protect yourself from gaslighting or other manipulative behavior that makes you second-guess your inner wisdom.

As I've mentioned elsewhere, developing a practice that helps you be more present is important to release the chaos and negative programming that can be so loud in our minds and control our feelings. When it comes to being in your own energy, presence is required. You can't be both numb to what you're feeling and attuned to your energy at the same time. Somatic practices like breathwork, movement, yoga, meditation, and being in nature can all help you to "come home" to the present moment and yourself. Coming back to yourself feels like a huge exhale when you didn't even know you were holding your breath. From there, you can begin to feel your way into higher frequencies of love, gratitude, and connection to self and others.

Dating without any awareness of the energetic connection between you and others is truly flying without a net. Without a connection to your own energy, sensing others will be an unconscious experience that can lead you astray, as we've already discussed. If you only pay attention to words, and the emotions they elicit, you will miss out on all the energetic information that's constantly being transmitted from and to you. Love is not an intellectual pursuit; you can't think yourself into choosing an amazing partner.

When it comes to manifesting true love, you could skip this book entirely and focus solely on understanding your energy. Some people search for love and others allow it to come to them. The ones who do the latter have a strong energetic alignment with the energy of love, and that stems from an alignment with self. Perhaps you've been that person, or you've witnessed this phenomenon in action. Back when I struggled to get dates, I looked with awe at my friends who seemed to effortlessly attract devoted romantic partners. *How do they do that?*

I would marvel. Even as my own energy began to shift, I didn't fully understand what was happening. Things just began to flow more easily for me romantically as I got out of my head and into my body (this coincided with discovering and falling in love with yoga), allowing myself to be more present.

It was by observing my clients up close that I began to understand the hidden power of energy in attraction. Through them I was able to give voice to what felt intuitive but was hard to explain. You are your most magnetic when you're the most true to who you are. I encourage you to look at your own life to see the evidence of how your sweet spot is squarely your own energy. Take the objective observations you make about yours and other people's vibes and humbly ask yourself: *What can I learn from this?* The answers you receive can change your life.

The Energetic Cost of Settling

"I feel like everything in my life is about to get better," said a client who'd broken up with a romantic partner who'd stonewalled and gaslit her for nearly two years. The same week she moved out of their shared apartment, she got an offer for a dream job she'd been vying for for nearly a year. A friend of a friend suddenly needed a housesitter for a months-long job relocation, giving her a comfortable and free place to stay while she found a new home. "Does this happen? Do people start manifesting when they get out of a bad relationship?" she asked me. The answer is yes—it's common for new opportunities and serendipities to arise when you put yourself in a better energetic state. The glow-up is real.

You get the love life you settle for. If you've wanted true love but settled for its pale imitations, you made the decision that was good enough. When you choose to be in a relationship, situationship, or friends-with-benefits-ship with someone who can't give you the love you want, you're settling. When you hold yourself back from intimate relationships because they feel too vulnerable, you're settling. We've all been there, but if you choose to stay there, at least acknowledge (with self-compassion) your choice and understand its energetic effects. Staying connected to unavailable people or cutting yourself off from love harms you because it normalizes the frequency of insecurity and emotional dysregulation caused by unmet needs.

All settling doesn't look the same. There are degrees, just as there are levels of relationships. If you're in a painful place in your romantic relationships, notice what you're settling for. When you go on a date with someone new, where does your energetic comfort lie? What is the treatment, the relationship dynamic, the behavior that doesn't sit well with your soul? Are you entertaining a toxic or lackluster relationship dynamic, all the while hoping it'll change? Or are you telling yourself you're still open to meeting the right person while simultaneously giving your energy to the wrong ones? Your attractions will give you huge clues to what is energetically familiar for you, even if the dynamics are unwanted. Become compassionately curious about how wide the gap is between the level of love your soul is craving and what your energy is drawn to.

You can't always know in advance how you'll benefit from your choice to walk away from what you don't want, even when there's a pull of attraction present. Cultivate courage by being honest with yourself about all the ways the wrong relationships are holding or have held you back in the past. Notice the thoughts or rationalizations that arise to justify settling. Feel the difference in your energy when you're in that dynamic versus when you're away from it. Do you feel lighter, more confident, more inspired? If so, that's a sign you're coming back to yourself and your own energy. The right relationship won't make you feel worse about yourself.

how to find true love

Love is more powerful than fear, but we must be brave in choosing it through our relationship choices. Stepping out on faith and into your power to feel more yourself is one of the most powerful choices you can make.

Heartwork

For more clarity on your current romantic frequency, answer the following (remember to use self-compassionate curiosity):

1. Do I know what my own energy feels like? If not, am I willing to discover it? What action(s) can I commit to in order to find or strengthen this connection to myself?
2. Beyond the physical or superficial, what am I effortlessly and consistently attracted to in a potential romantic partner?
3. What consistent qualities do my romantic partners or crushes possess that I want in future partners?
4. What consistent qualities do my romantic partners or crushes possess that I DON'T want in future partners?
5. Who do I know who has a strong relationship pattern that serves them well? What can I learn from what they must believe and feel to manifest that pattern?
6. Who do I know who has a strong relationship pattern that doesn't serve them? What can I learn from what they must believe and feel to manifest that pattern?
7. How have the love beliefs I identified in chapter 6 shown up in my romantic frequency (what I effortlessly attract/ am attracted to)?

CHAPTER 10

allow the universe
to assist you

Many people are dating the hard way. Not just the hard way, but also the hardest way, with no connection at all to spirit or to a higher love. At some point you must decide for yourself how you think the universe works, and what you believe about the true nature of love. If you believe, as I do, that love is infinitely abundant, now's the time to act accordingly. If you believe, as I do, that the universe wants you to have true love (why would your soul have such a deep desire for it otherwise?), then you're in luck. Now you can get excited about discovering how and when it'll happen for you. It's safe to say it will happen in ways that you couldn't have predicted. Which is part of the magic of life and love.

If you believe the universe is completely random—or worse, out to get you—I encourage you to reconsider your position. When I speak of making true love inevitable, it isn't because I have the perfect hack to get someone to propose marriage in 30 days, or because your challenging life circumstances have no relevance to your dating experience. *Inevitability* is only something a higher love can achieve, with your cooperation and co-creation. We don't have the power of inevitability—the universe does. Love does. Going forward, we'll talk about the ways you can allow the universe to carry you over your circumstances to true love.

Have you ever noticed that some people seem to have a personal magic that allows them to attract good things and people into their lives with greater ease than others? In relationships, it's obvious that some people expect more and seem to get it, while others want more, but struggle despite their efforts. You can chalk it up to random luck, but if you look closer, you might notice there seems to be a greater factor at play. This may feel like a little too much for you to get on board with, and if so, I invite you to reflect on the miracles you've witnessed in your own life. If you've never considered the spiritual aspect of your love journey, stick with me here and see what might resonate with you.

The Spiritual Nature of Your Love Journey

If you didn't pick this up in the previous chapter, I believe love is spiritual. Many overlook this simple truth. Who can blame them given our cultural discomfort with the nature of spirit? Popular culture praises the intellect over the soul.

Transcendence is only possible because of the nature of spirit. Unlike our physical reality, it is unlimited. The first step in transcending unwanted romantic circumstances is to embrace the spiritual aspect of your love journey. You were born with a soul; it wasn't something you acquired along the way. Why would you have a soul if it didn't have a reason for existing? Your desire for a soulmate to do life with comes from this essential part of you.

Here's what we know: (1) life is clearly here for us to be in a state of continued growth, and (2) we have a soul. The intensely compelling nature of love (and romantic love, specifically) leads me to believe our soul's growth is the whole point of true love. On the deepest level of who we are, we're always being guided to a higher level of love.

Honor the Role of Self-Love

So how do we connect more to our soul, and its wisdom and power? In the last chapter, we covered the energetic aspect of connecting to yourself. Self-love also has a major role to play. Love is always the portal to any manifestation that's in our highest good. Romantic relationships are often the most emotionally intimate relationships we have outside of early childhood. What shows up for you romantically is a really powerful manifestation of where you are on your self-love journey. Looking honestly at where you are right now can be scary and hard. That's why self-compassion is step 1 in the Self-Love Formula. As I always remind my clients, if fully loving yourself was easy, everyone would do it and hardly anyone does.

As mentioned, there's a hard way to navigate dating and there's an easier way. Easier doesn't always mean *easy*, but you don't have to go on this journey alone. The easier way to true love begins with your sincere intention to transcend anything unloving in your approach to love.

The Easier Way, Part 1: Intention

In his best-selling book *The Seat of the Soul*[1], author Gary Zukav describes intention as a universal force. Like creativity, inspiration, joy, and love, it is something that exists, period. An artist taps into, or channels, creativity. They do not have to "create" creativity; they only need to ready themselves to receive it internally. Similarly, love is not something you have to worry about somehow generating externally; your spiritual assignment is to activate the endless reserve of love inside you and allow it to inspire and carry you.

1 Gary Zukav, *The Seat of the Soul* (Simon & Schuster, 2014).

how to find true love

Intention makes inspiration, serendipity, and clarity much easier to come by. By tapping into the power of intention, you will 100 percent get results. Something will always be returned to you by that choice—cause and effect is a spiritual law as much as a physical one. If you drop a glass, gravity will take care of the rest. If you set a sincere intention, something unseen happens that sets your intention in motion.

Setting an intention is not a guarantee of getting what you want. Maybe, if the multiverse theory of the universe is correct, you eventually will, somewhere in time. But on this timeline of your current life as the reader of this book, it's up to you to do your part. Luckily, intention helps you with your assignment.

Setting Intentions

Intention is how you hit "start route" in your spiritual GPS. An intention is something that you plan to achieve. It's not merely a wish or a hope; it's a decision. We've all seen enough courtroom trials on television to know that "intent" can be the difference between a life sentence and an acquittal. In life, just as in TV lawyer shows, intention matters. Here's how to effectively set intentions to support your love journey:

1. **Clarify the vision:** What is your highest wish for the romantic love you want? It could be to live a life of joy and abundance with a romantic partner. Or to experience deep emotional and physical intimacy in a true love relationship. Tweak the vision you began articulating in chapter 8 until it resonates with you on an emotional level. If it makes your soul feel good, it's in your highest good.

2. **What comes next?:** Once you set a high-level intention, it's your responsibility to do what you can to align yourself with what you're manifesting. Remember, that is your ultimate assignment on your path to true love. Use

intention to help guide you toward your next best steps on this journey. Imagine that you're energetically in New York and your future relationship is in California, heading your way. Sure, you could stay in New York and hope California finds you (it will eventually, but it might take a while). Or you could start heading west to meet it in the middle. How to reach that "middle" on your love journey is an answer that intention will reveal if you ask it to.

3. **Use the first person:** Write your love intentions down using the first person—for example, *I choose to manifest feeling the abundance of love inside me* is more emotionally resonant than a list of intentions without an "I" statement.

4. **Ask for what you want, not what you don't:** For instance, *I set an intention to stop dating unavailable people* is focused on what you don't want—unavailable people. Beyond stopping an old behavior, what would you rather do? A more empowering option is: *I set an intention to only date people who are emotionally and physically available to me.*

The Easier Way, Part 2: Gratitude

If there is a cheat code to the energy and emotion of both love and joy, it's gratitude. This superpower brings improvements to our emotional, physical, and mental health. And of course, our energy. Study after study has concluded what we can observe in our own lives—gratitude and joy go hand in hand.

Joy is the frequency of abundance. The more of it we experience, the more goodness flows to and through us. Gratitude is a practice of looking for and acknowledging the good in any moment. It is the antidote to blaming and shaming. You can't feel both shame and gratitude at the same time, as Brené Brown points out. It truly is a gift—a powerful manifestation of love that brings inner peace and satisfaction. And the best part? You have the power to choose it at any time, in any place, in the face of any circumstance. Like love, gratitude is a choice. It's not dependent on *feeling* grateful. Sometimes feelings of gratitude arise naturally from insights or serendipitous outcomes. Gratitude fuels those moments of grace and makes them more prevalent in our lives. It's that powerful. Other times, we must make a concerted effort to turn our lens toward gratitude. What you focus on expands, and gratitude is (thankfully) no exception.

Strengthening Gratitude

Here are some simple practices you can do to improve your practice of gratitude, any time, any place:

Daily gratitude: A daily ritual, such as a gratitude journal or simply taking time each day to meditate on the love inside you, helps to strengthen an overall "attitude of gratitude."

Meditation/prayer: Intentions, mantras, and prayers of gratitude can be used as they feel inspiring and heart-opening to you. If your soul loves it, that's your green light.

Journaling: Any regular journaling practice can incorporate your observations of and thoughts on gratitude, love, and/or simply allow the space for processing emotions.

Documenting grateful moments: Were you able to tap into gratitude in a challenging moment? Acknowledge yourself and the loving choice that made that possible.

Expressing gratitude in your relationships: It's easy to take for granted that people know you're grateful for them. Making an effort to communicate and receive more gratitude in your current relationships is its own gratitude practice, one that will deepen the love in your life.

Self-gratitude: In the Self-Love Formula, I asked you to choose something that makes you uniquely you that you're grateful for.

Here's your self-gratitude reminder. In your practice of gratitude, don't forget about you.

The Easier Way, Part 3: Surrender

Far from giving up, surrender is about relinquishing the illusion of control. It's an illusion, because the only thing in the universe you can truly control is yourself, and doing that is a big enough challenge most of the time! Since we're constantly discovering new aspects of ourselves (scientifically and spiritually), it's safe to say we don't have all the answers about the unknowable forces behind our existence. Given our desire to control what, when, and where things happen for us romantically, surrender isn't always an easy choice. But it's worth doing if you want to use your energy effectively—that's the easier way.

Your Department vs. the Universe's Department

In chapter 7, we first discussed this concept of your department vs. the universe's department. We're revisiting it here as a reminder of the importance of focusing your energy in productive ways. The anxiety that dating can trigger or exacerbate is caused by resistance to and fear of the unknown. When we're triggered by uncertainty, an unconscious response might be to ruminate over unanswerable questions like, *What will happen next?* You can't know that answer. Life is nothing if not unpredictable. Which is why anxiety, while completely normal and human, is also a sign that your energy is being misdirected, or split.

Cause and effect is a universal law—everything that happens is a result of something that caused it to happen. You might not know why the tree fell, but there were causes that preceded it. From our tiny, individual vantage point, we can't know all of the levels of causation that will bring your intention for a true love partnership to fruition. You can't know where you will meet your person. You can't know when you'll meet them, or guarantee how, or reliably predict who they will be. All of those unknowns are out of your control. As such, they fall under the "universe's department." What you do to prepare yourself for when they show up falls under "your department." You've got enough to do to get ready to recognize, receive, and reciprocate true love. Don't spin your wheels trying (and failing) to do the universe's job instead of your own.

Here's a mantra to use for support: *I don't know how, I don't know when, I don't know where. I only know that I will meet an amazing partner.*

Cultivate Patience

Patience becomes easier when you relinquish your attempts to control the universe's department. By doing your own work, you'll see the benefits in how you think and feel about yourself and about love. Your ability to navigate your love journey with patience is also increased with the cultivation of the following:

- **Joy:** Rather than waiting for a future moment to be joyful, find ways to experience more joy now. What lights you up? What are you feeling called to experience more of? What or who are you finally ready to let go of? That's your inner wisdom guiding you to a more joyful place. Listen to it!

- **Faith:** *Do I believe the universe wants me to live a life full of love? Do I believe true love is available to me?* As I mentioned at the start of this chapter, you must decide for yourself what you believe about love and your ability to have it. As we've covered at length, what you believe matters. A lot. Check in with yourself on these fundamental questions. Don't try to convince yourself to have faith—allow yourself to see it at work in life.

- **Noticing divine timing at work:** Pay attention to how timing works. Notice how many things you wanted on *your time* that came into your life on the *universe's time*. How much better is the universe at timing than you are? As Oprah Winfrey says: "God can dream a bigger dream for you than you can dream for yourself." Which means that you and God/spirit/universe are not necessarily working on the same timeline. And that's actually a beautiful thing.

- **Mindfulness:** Practicing mindfulness—staying aware and in the present—will assist you greatly on your love journey. Meditation, journaling, breathwork, movement—there are many modalities that help you to become more present and attuned to your thoughts, feelings, and energy. Commit to developing a more holistic awareness of how you're experiencing life; including your relationship with your technology and social media.

- **Honor your intuition:** Your intuition is like a muscle—the more you exercise it, the stronger it grows. What are the whispers, the nudges, the gut feelings you're noticing? Not just when it comes to love, but all things in your life. Intuition is how the universe nudges you in the right direction. If you're serious about finding true love, I encourage you to listen.

- **Cultivate your love confidence:** In chapter 5, you learned the importance of having the confidence to know you can handle love. Your love confidence is firmly in the category of "your department." As a reminder—perfect confidence isn't required, but increased confidence is attainable as well as extremely helpful.

The Easier Way, Part 4: Serendipity

The existence of the universal force of serendipity is a consistent source of gratitude in my life. Each serendipitous event is a little miracle that just pops up, seemingly out of nowhere. Always in such an unguessable way. What could be more delightful? We all experience serendipities, big and small. As a student and fan of serendipity, I've noticed the biggest ones tend to have certain hallmarks. I see it in my clients, who tend to "randomly" meet future partners once they're feeling more relaxed and excited about dating.

Being in your energy, instead of fear, worry, or the vicissitudes of dating culture, increases your alignment with love and therefore serendipity. Practicing intention, gratitude, and surrender increases your serendipity mojo. Here are a few more things to help you court the serendipity that will lead you to your true love partnership:

1. **Follow the breadcrumbs:** Who's been on your mind? What's that place you keep driving past and have been meaning to go? Say yes to that last-minute invite out of your comfort zone. Go take that pottery class, just because you want to. Take a trip across town or the continent because there's something about that place that's always intrigued you. You don't need a better reason than you're feeling called to do it.

2. **Notice broken patterns:** Did your toxic ex finally get the message and leave you alone? Did you establish a boundary that held? Did you make an unexpected and delightful new connection for the first time in 30 years? A pattern breaking is a signal of a big energy shift in your life. Pay attention to the extra energy swirling (opportunities, relationships, feeling excited) and be on the lookout—things are happening!

3. **Observe how things come to you:** Do good things happen when you're making your art? Or spending time with friends? Maybe serendipities show up more when you're taking better physical care of yourself. Use your past wins

to fuel your future successes, as my friend, author, and icon Bevy Smith would say.

4. **Decide everything has meaning:** The rubber-meets-the-road moment on the other side of an energetic upgrade is when you hit an emotional pothole. Re-center yourself with the knowledge that it has meaning. Your department is to discover it. Whether you're disappointed because you didn't meet anyone at a party or that the person you met ghosted you, find the meaning. A great question for reflection is: *If this situation happened to teach me something in my highest good, what might that be?*

Engaging the power of serendipity on your love journey isn't just about the moment of meeting your partner on an airplane. Any series of seemingly unrelated events can bring you to that spot. You could run into your college roommate in November who recommends a new show, and at that show three weeks later, you run into your neighbor who mentions their company is hiring for a position in Chicago. You might decide to interview for it, because you've recently been thinking about how much you love Chicago. In March, after many rounds of interviewing, you might get flown to your final interview at the company headquarters in Chicago. Maybe you don't wind up taking the job, but you move to Chicago anyway because you met your soulmate on the flight and that's where they live.

Albert Einstein is quoted as saying: "I think the most important question facing humanity is, 'Is the universe a friendly place?'" My answer to that question is an emphatic yes, and I'd argue that serendipity proves it. Hopefully you can observe the power of these universal forces and energies in your own life. And hopefully you're feeling more supported and equipped to transcend dating the hard way with the help of the universe.

Heartwork

Reflect on the following:

1. Are you able to see love as spiritual and abundant? What resistance might you have to this perspective? Are you willing to challenge any ideas that love is scarce and something you must control?
2. Do you feel you've been doing things the easier or harder way on your love journey? Which way do you choose going forward, and what does that look like for you?
3. What intentions are you prepared to set for this next phase of your love journey?
4. Are you willing to commit to a gratitude practice to support you? What does that look like?
5. What are your thoughts on surrender? Do you see how it can serve you? Why or why not?
6. Is serendipity something you can observe in your own life? What are some of the most serendipitous events that have occurred for you?

STEP 4

date in alignment with love (skillset)

CHAPTER 11

let true love in

Y ou can't love another person without loving yourself" is a misleading statement. Loving other people isn't usually our difficulty. Trusting, communicating, maintaining boundaries, etc.—those can be challenges for us to confront, but *feeling* love isn't hard. Regardless of how much it might seem otherwise, your primary love assignment is to learn to receive. We are only compatible with partners who withhold love if that's what we do to ourselves.

Can You Accept a Compliment?

You know those days when you don't feel your most attractive? Your hair isn't cooperating, you're wearing an ill-fitting outfit, or you can see bags under your eyes from a sleepless night? When someone gives you a compliment on a day like that, do you suddenly love your hair or outfit? Probably not. Even accepting "That color looks great on you" from a friend can be difficult when all you can see is how tired you look, or the ways in which you think your body is lacking. How many compliments have you deflected or diminished because you couldn't see the truth of it, and therefore didn't believe anyone else could?

Just as receiving a sincere compliment from a person you trust can be hard, letting love in from someone new isn't always easy. Love, as my friend Amari Ice says, "is the ultimate compliment." If you've ever experienced a deep romantic connection, you know that the reality of it can be scary. Logically, it might seem the thing we want the most—to be unconditionally loved for who we really are—would be welcomed with open arms. But we are not as logical as we like to think we are. My clients usually have their biggest freak-outs when they finally make the kind of authentic romantic connection they've been seeking for years.

It's counterintuitive for most of us to imagine love is waiting on *us* to be ready for *it*—but it is. Letting love into your mind, heart, and spirit might take some work. Allowing yourself to be physically intimate with someone new might be challenging. You've already begun the work of transcending any romantic challenge by reading this book. Each new level of love and intimacy you reach will require you to expand your capacity to handle it. Let the evidence of how far you've already come inspire you to keep going and growing.

Open Your Heart

Your mind has the power to open and close your heart. Your confidence in love will dictate how much your conscious and subconscious mind allows you to open up. Giving someone the "cold shoulder" is a way of closing your heart. Perhaps you also know that sometimes, once you shut it, opening it again can feel impossible, even when you want to. Ego and shame can keep us at a distance from love. Ever wanted to apologize or wish you could take back something you said in anger, only to find yourself frozen, unable to speak? How about losing interest in someone once you've won them over or realized they actually like you? If you've been on the other side—having someone's affections cut off, seemingly out of the blue—you know how impenetrable a once openhearted person can become, seemingly in an instant.

As Michael Singer teaches in his book *The Untethered Soul*[1], if you can close your heart, you can also open it again if you're determined enough. Transcending the struggles of modern dating requires taking insecurity and fear less personally—yours and other people's. The scarier it feels to open your heart fully, the more committed you must be to doing just that. The power of intention to let more love circulate in and out will reveal the new actions required. You might notice, for instance, that when a friend asks how you've been, you default to saying "fine" when in truth, you've been having a hard time. Or a great time! Even a seemingly small thing like being more open with your friends helps you to create a more openhearted new normal.

You Are Qualified for Love

It's my repeated observation and firm belief that nothing disqualifies you or anyone else from having true love. Your belief to the contrary and your capacity to receive can certainly block you from love, but disqualify you? Never. If you can agree that love is infinitely abundant inside of you and everyone else, then what can disqualify you from having it?

The love coach in me always groans when I hear people regurgitate disempowering dating statistics. I know statistics aren't destiny, but to many they're "evidence" of their worst love fears. You will be best served by anchoring yourself in a higher truth than appearances suggest.

1 Michael A. Singer, *The Untethered Soul: The Journey Beyond Yourself* (New Harbinger/ Noetic, 2007).

how to find true love

In chapter 6, I mentioned the belief some Black women hold that by virtue of their race and gender, they're less desirable as romantic partners. I hear this a lot from clients and I'm never surprised. I am well aware of the data and lived experience that informs this belief.[2] And yet, as discussed in chapter 10, fundamentally we must ask ourselves, "What do I believe about the universe?" Or God, or the creator, or source ... whatever it is you think caused our world and our lives to exist. Whatever label you give that life force, do you think *it* discriminates? If you're historically marginalized or discriminated against, you are being called to a higher level of faith than the world acknowledges. You might be a Black woman, or a trans man, or a plus-sized person in a fat-phobic world. Will people discriminate against you? It's quite possible, or even likely.

That reflects their poor life choices, and clear evidence they aren't your people. But, on the level of spirit, do you think love is inherently less available to you? Are you doomed to a life without the love your heart is aching for? Are you stuck in a scarcity mindset because you assume you know exactly the age, height, color, educational level, and hobbies of your romantic options? Love is abundant, but as we've discussed, if you narrow your desires to a height preference, income level, or any other rigid category, those humans are finite. If this is what you want, you have to accept that you might never find it all.

What is most important to you—true love or a high-status incarnation of an ideal partner? There's no "wrong" answer, but your answer does matter. How open to true love are you? These are questions you must decide for yourself. As a Black woman, I rejected the notion years ago that the universe has marked me as unlucky or unlovable. Love is bigger than that. I've personally done what I've seen countless other Black women do, which is to decide: My color

---

2 Kiara Byrd, "Black Women, AI, and the Dating App Dilemma," *Essence*, April 15, 2024, https://www.essence.com/lifestyle/dating-apps-black-women/.

does not disqualify me from having the love I want. And we've manifested true love accordingly.

Separate Painful Lies from Spiritual Truth

Imagine a child who is born into the painful and unfair circumstances of being unwanted by their family of origin. To make matters worse, in seen and unseen ways, they are repeatedly lied to about their worth and made to feel like they aren't enough. Horrible, right? Now imagine this child, all grown up and doing their best to navigate life with a constant, fearful voice of those early lies in their head. That voice of negativity and fear could easily feel like the absolute truth. Who could blame them? But to us, with the benefit of objectivity and compassion for that mistreated child, *we* can see the lies it tells.

Now, what would happen when someone comes into their life, with a heart full of unconditional love for this person? For a romantic partnership no less, one of the most emotionally triggering experiences we can possibly have? In the fantasy version of love, their wounds are instantly healed and they're able to believe and accept this new version of reality.

I probably don't have to tell you how hard it would be for that person to feel worthy or comfortable with letting love in. Would you expect this person to have a series of romantically healthy relationships *without* going through an inner transformation? For that to happen (and it would be 100% possible through the power of love), that person's entire relationship with their inner voice would have to change.

Maybe you know someone like that, or you recognize some aspects of this hypothetical person within yourself. In my experience, we all can relate to some degree. The inside job of love is to make enough space mentally, emotionally, and spiritually to let it in. To make love your new and complete normal. To release control and allow the power of love to surprise you.

how to find true love

Stop Managing Circumstances

The definition of *transcend* is to rise or extend above or beyond ordinary limits. At present, we are in a collective state of romantic limitation. As discussed in the previous chapter, there is an easier way to navigate your love journey, and there is a harder way. It's easy to observe that most people are going the very hard way. You can either manage the circumstances of modern dating, or you can transcend them. My hope for you is to choose transcendence.

For millions of people, their agency and confidence in finding love, if they ever had it, has been lost by a dating industry motivated by making as much money as possible for its shareholders. The people hoping to use dating apps to quickly find romantic partners and delete the app for good are at a disadvantage based on these misaligned incentives.

A simple analogy involves a common sentiment I've heard frustrated daters express: *The dating pool has pee in it.* Let's assume that's true—the proverbial "pee" being toxicity, superficiality, scammers, time wasters, and the like. The hard way of "swimming" in this pool is to invest in goggles, or perhaps a full-body wet suit, or to convince yourself that while not ideal, you'd rather swim in the tainted waters than opt out entirely.

Much of modern dating advice is centered around this approach—you may see some "experts" say things like, "I will teach you easy steps to escape the pool as quickly as possible" if you will. This is the realm of "say these 5 things to make them want you" and "the 5 dating app photos to make yourself irresistible" type advice. No offense to anyone who teaches this approach—it absolutely can be helpful to give daters some framework to follow when they're floundering. At the start of my love career, I gave a lot of this "circumstance management" guidance to help my clients on the harder path. This kind of advice often doesn't work because you can't hack your way out of dating challenges by external tactics alone.

Inevitability is something only a higher love can achieve. On the spectrum of love to fear, any belief that you must, for example, say the "perfect" thing, have the "perfect" body, or have the most romantic options in order to find a great partner is squarely on the fear end. Rather than play by fear's rules, a choice to transcend gives you the power of love to assist you.

What "Being Open" to Love Means

You already know there is a choice between being open to love and being closed. You have either been closed to romance yourself or have witnessed someone who was. They manage to energetically remove themselves from the realm of romantic possibility. In strong cases of this, you can energetically sense their protective vibe. We can get really good at finding ways to keep love at bay.

If you're single and you've been making an effort to date, or going on dates, you might feel like you are totally open to love. But if you're being honest (and I hope you will be honest with yourself—when done with kindness, honesty is an act of love), you can probably observe the ways you close yourself off, even just a little. A lot of this is completely practical—if you are only attracted to women, for instance, you might be closed to being approached romantically by men. However, this tendency goes way beyond this type of pragmatic, or even conscious choice. It's only with the benefit of an objective view of many others that I am able to detect these "closures" or "blocks" in action. They stealthily hide in plain sight.

If It's Hysterical, It's Historical

Why is dating such an emotional experience? Why do we feel so over-whelmed at times as we navigate our intimate relationships? Because romantic relationships are the perfect forum for your oldest wounds to get poked. I'm not a fan of the term "self-sabotage" because it seems to miss the point. We're not trying to actively hurt ourselves; we're trying to maintain our status quo. To keep ourselves "safe" from new, expansive experiences. You will get triggered if you go deep enough, or if the wound is fresh enough. A trigger is a non-event unless there's a bullet in the chamber.

You and your partner(s) each come to your relationship with pro-verbial bullets in your chambers. For the purposes of making true love your reality, being triggered is actually a hidden gift. Alice (see chapter 6) learned from her reaction to her breakup with Trevor that she had been carrying a core belief that she would never experience unconditional love. Only by facing it head-on could she move on to changing it for good.

Whatever triggered you in a romantic relationship might have been unacceptable, painful, or completely innocuous. Regardless, if you don't understand that it's *your* bullet responding, you might think your partner shot you. "If it's hysterical, it's historical" is one of my favorite sayings, as it reminds me to stay clear on what's really happening. These wounds are deep and you might never fully understand their origin. That's okay. You can heal from the past without identifying every single past trauma. They don't disqualify you from the love you want in the future—nothing does.

Windfalls of Love

In chapter 7, I introduced the concept of a "windfall" of love. Like windfalls of money, windfalls of love are a real phenomenon. Have you ever met someone and felt an instant mutual romantic connection that takes you both by surprise? You might not experience them often, but there are occasional moments in life when they break through, seemingly out of nowhere. That's what happens when a deep romantic connection shows up in your life. It might take you a moment to recognize its significance (love often shows up in ways or at times you don't expect). But once you acknowledge your feelings, its uniqueness becomes undeniable.

In my opinion and experience, we all get at least a few windfalls of love throughout our lives. Openness to allowing love to take center stage and flourish in all of your relationships increases your chances at windfalls of romantic love. Some people get multiple great loves in their lives. It might appear that others never get any—but I don't think that's true. I've heard many stories of regret from people who weren't ready or available to receive that love when it showed up. Maybe they were with someone else at the time, or it wasn't the kind of person they imagined themselves with, or they were just too freaked out by the intensity of their feeling. But that's okay. While we often squander our windfalls of love (like lottery winners and cash), the good news is you keep getting chances. Love is always making its way to you.

Let Others See You

In order to be truly loved for who you are, you must be seen. To be seen as who you really are, you must be brave enough to be yourself. If you know who you are and how valuable you are, then letting others see you becomes easier, and possibly easy. It might even become your favorite thing in life when you're seen by the right person.

There are many single people who don't want to be single who are hiding in plain sight. On dating apps and social media, they're hiding behind filters, outdated or AI-generated photos, clichés, and whatever their "comfortable thing" is. For instance, some people are comfortable being sexy, or being seen as smart, or as a talented artist. These comfortable little bubbles we occupy are sometimes what's holding us back.

What does it mean to you to be more visible? Do you speak up more often than not? Put more (or less) effort into your appearance? Toss your hat into the ring for a big promotion at work? Go on a date? There are so many ways the idea of being seen might be relevant to you right now. It could be as basic as deleting your old photos and taking new ones, embracing how you look today versus 5 years ago. That's powerful action aligned with what you want.

What to Expect When You're Expanding

There's a lot of emotion tied up in the energy and beliefs we hold. When you start to crack open the old energy, the feelings will start flowing. Other things in your life might start to shift, and even fall away. Change happens in predictable and unpredictable ways. When your next windfall of love arrives, more old energy gets shaken up. It's a beautiful experience, and it can also be emotionally disregulating.

Thankfully, when you invest in your relationship with yourself, you're able to develop the skill of receiving love. Windfalls of love don't happen every day, but they will happen to you if that is your intention and you are willing to be brave. Any past challenges you might have had with receiving love aren't your destiny. Hold the vision of the love you deserve in your heart and trust that when you are ready to receive that depth of connection, it will arrive.

Avoidance is a love block because of its energetic and emotional signature: *I can't handle letting love in.* Strengthening your comfort with your emotions will prepare you to know on a deep level—*I am ready to let love in.* The cocktail of brain and energetic chemistry when you allow someone to see you can be destabilizing, as you're feeling so much all at once. Observe your particular patterns of freakout in these instances without judgment.

Instead, choose action over attraction: Your chemistry radar is recalibrating, and at first it's likely to draw you to the same dynamics you're used to. It's up to you to say no to people who reinforce the old beliefs and yes to the new energy. Don't worry—remember that your attractions will shift over time. This doesn't mean you should date someone you're not attracted to. But you should date against your type with an open heart and mind. It doesn't take long to feel differently about yourself with the evidence new actions present.

Set the intention to see the evidence you need: Think you're too _____ to find love? Right now, you can choose the sincere intention to see evidence that you're wrong. Considering the possibility of something new is powerful enough in itself, and setting an intention makes it show up faster.

Heartwork

Reflect on the following:

1. How well can I receive a compliment? Do I believe people mean the kind or flattering things they say to me? Am I willing to start saying "thank you" rather than deflect, even when it feels uncomfortable to do so?

2. Do I believe the universe/God/source places the same limits on love as society does? Have I put limits on the love that's possible for me in the past?

3. What, if anything, do I think disqualifies a person from true love? Am I willing to consider that I do have the power to make true love a natural and inevitable result of my inner alignment with love?

4. How emotionally triggering is romantic love and dating for me? Am I able to practice self-compassion and allow myself to heal from old wounds?

5. Have I been as open to love as I've told myself I am? What does being more open look like for me going forward?
6. How can I mentally and emotionally prepare myself for the experience of letting more love in? Am I ready to embrace the discomfort of more vulnerability?

CHAPTER 12

discover your dating archetype

Am I too picky or not picky enough? Does attraction grow over time? How do I judge compatibility? Should I sleep with them right away, or wait a set amount of time? How do I communicate my boundaries? How do I know who to trust? Are all the good ones taken? What does this emoji mean—is that a yes? How long will it take for me to meet my person? Should I give up entirely on actively trying to meet someone?

Frustration, impatience, confusion, hopelessness...All common emotions that most everyone seems to experience in varying degrees when it comes to dating. When not going well, dating can be an isolating endeavor, one that feels like you're uniquely challenged and maybe even doomed to failure. Even if you find others whose experience you can relate to, the comfort that "miserable company" can provide doesn't necessarily lead to clarity on how to do better. Luckily, your feelings, while valid, are not facts.

Take heart in the knowledge you are far from alone. This grand social experiment of dating is both deeply personal and connected to everyone else—if it's happening to you, it's happening to others as well. In this chapter, you'll learn about the dating archetypes I've created to help you make sense of your experience and to know how to date better going forward.

How the Archetypes Work

Avoider, Looper, Surfer, and Sailor. Before we dive into these four archetypes, please note that yours isn't a permanent state if you don't want it to be. Please do not take them on as your identity or your destiny. Think of them as a snapshot of where you are right now and how best to move forward on your path toward true love. They're designed to help you gain clarity on the state of your dating (or non-dating) life. When used without self-judgment (remember to ground in self-compassionate curiosity), learning about your current archetype will assist you in growing more love confident and effective in your dating efforts.

The Avoider
Romantic frequency: Closed, insecure

The name says it all—you avoid dating or talking about dating, and yet you think about dating and your desire for romance. A loving partnership might be something you deeply desire, but your actions rarely, if ever, reflect it. This phase doesn't generally include people who are taking an intentional break; it's more about those who actively avoid dating. All of the archetypes can persist for years or even decades, but the Avoider phase can be especially lengthy if not intentionally interrupted.

The Avoider phase can look like the following:

- Not dating at all
- Not acknowledging any romantic desire

- Acknowledging desire, but feeling unable or unwilling to act on it
- Having intense crushes on unavailable partners who aren't interested and/or aren't single
- Starting and quickly stopping on dating apps
- Browsing on apps but never going on dates
- Feeling at a complete loss as to how to jump-start your love life

It takes some effort to keep love at bay, and Avoiders (consciously or unconsciously) do so by:

- allowing fear or disappointment to become a justification for not trying romantically;
- wishing for an out-of-the-blue "lightning strike" of love to pass through their defenses;
- keeping busy with work, travel, doing for others, and generally overextending themselves;
- not allowing sufficient time or space for self-care and rest;
- telling themselves that at some point in the future, they'll be ready to be proactive about love;
- focusing on all the reasons why dating will be/is hard/futile;
- using "fantasy as a crutch" (as discussed in chapter 2).

Typical Avoider client complaint: "I never meet anyone."

You might feel like a romantic misfit, but typically Avoiders are the whole package without knowing it. What lies on the other side of your romantic deprivation is an abundance of love. Avoiders will typically attract people who are into them but either can't notice or will find a way to discount/dismiss their interest.

The Looper

Romantic frequency: Mixed, disempowered

If you're a Looper, you're stuck in that dreaded dating loop or pattern you don't want. Loopers bravely "put themselves out there" and might date prolifically, but their love lives resemble a *Groundhog Day* pattern of the same dynamics happening over and over.

Loopers keep the cycle going by:

- saying yes to the same kinds of people and dynamics over and over;
- blaming others for their romantic outcomes (e.g., "I keep attracting narcissists");
- focusing on external characteristics over demonstrable availability and relationship skills (e.g., dating someone because they "check boxes" and overlooking red flags);
- being more focused on being in a relationship than co-creating the right relationship;
- treating dating as a "numbers game";
- not understanding their power to say no even when and especially when they have chemistry, but little else.

Typical Looper client complaint: "I have no idea how to find someone who actually wants a relationship."

Loopers have no shortage of people ready to date them, but it's hard for them to see their own love blocks. As you learned in chapter 6, your romantic attractions aren't random. Since they can feel that way, Loopers unconsciously find themselves drawn to people whose blocks are a "puzzle piece" fit for their own self-belief.

The Surfer

Romantic frequency: Passionate, ambivalent

Surfers are true romantics guided by chemistry. They love the thrill of a new romantic connection and are usually good (consciously or unconsciously) at generating the spark of attraction. Surfers tend to "ride the wave" of chemistry, hoping or expecting that a strong attraction will result in a lasting relationship. A Surfer can get lucky with this strategy, but they also risk "wiping out" and experiencing a painful low that's the exact opposite of the intoxicating high they initially felt.

Surfers tend to:

- have an "I know when I know" attitude about attraction, regardless of how wrong they might have been in the past;
- interpret attraction as compatibility;
- dive into relationships quickly and intensely, not always taking time to get to know each other;
- be seduced by "love bombing" and grand gestures that feel romantic and "like a movie";
- need big breaks between relationships to nurse a broken or disappointed heart.

Typical Surfer client complaint: "We had an electric connection, and then it just fell apart."

Surfers are magnetic and open to connection, which is wonderful. The challenge is they love the dopamine hit of intensity, such as the start of a new relationship, more than they love (or are familiar with) consistency. Surfers can sometimes mistake infatuation for love and be attracted to people who also get high on the peaks and valleys of passion.

The Sailor

Romantic frequency: Empowered, love confident

On the love journey, the Sailor knows they are the captain of their ship. They have a comfort with/expectation of romantic commitment and can easily attract partners who want to commit to them. Others might view you as a "serial monogamist" or a "relationship person."

Typical Sailor client complaint: "I've been in relationships nonstop since I was sixteen. I don't even know who I am outside of being a couple."

Some Sailors are born that way, and some have gotten to this phase intentionally. Either way, Sailors have an uncanny ability to attract and be attracted to relationship-minded people. Being on the outside looking in, it can seem perplexing to non-Sailors how they manage to always find someone to partner with. The Sailor challenge can be in knowing who to choose, and not simply jumping in with someone who chooses them.

Your Attractions Change as You Do

Looking back over your life, you can likely see that over time, your attractions have changed. Often people will express to me their concern that they're not attracted to available people or that their habitual attractions are their forever destiny. This is not how attraction works. Chemistry is drawing you to people who match your inner love program; when that program changes, so do the people you have chemistry with.

Romantic Assignment by Archetype

When you're in a place of confusion about your dating life, the way forward is through understanding what love is asking of you. When you embrace your love journey as an important, lifelong exploration designed to teach you how to be more skilled at love, this makes complete sense. Frustration, pessimism, or despair can take root without this deeper perspective.

You learned about setting love intentions in chapter 10, and now you can apply that knowledge to set more specific, shorter-term goals that serve you on the path to your highest romantic intention—true love. If you are, for instance, squarely in an Avoider phase, telling yourself that you'll be ready for love when the right person shows up and magically breaks through your walls, you're taking a huge gamble. If you're not comfortable receiving romantic attention, you will freak out when someone shows up ready, able, and willing to love you for who you are.

Impatience is its own kind of love block, one that can actively stall you from moving forward. Take the time to understand your "love program" and then take effective action, rather than hoping to get lucky.

Here's how to understand what your next best step is on the path to true love. For all archetypes, ask yourself the following:

- Where am I now on my dating journey? Do I resonate with this description of my archetype or another? In what way(s)?
- How can I set myself up to win by getting closer to true love? Do I need to focus on a mindset (how I think about love), heartset (how I feel/what I believe about love and myself), soulset (how much faith I have in a higher love), or skillset (how to connect/choose aligned partners/move the relationship forward)? Or a combination?

- If I'm being honest, what is one thing I habitually do that is keeping me from moving forward?
- What evidence do I need to see right now to help me believe that I am making progress in love?

The Avoider Assignment

Good news—it's easy to move out of this phase. When you start acknowledging your desire for partnership and going on dates—voilà! You're no longer avoiding. The bottom line if you're an Avoider is to gain confidence in yourself and your ability to transcend whatever struggles have held you back until now. Your love life will begin to change once you become more determined and more courageous in opening your heart.

Tips for the Avoider:

- Pay attention to what else you are avoiding when it comes to your overall life satisfaction. What do you need to thrive as the most openhearted version of you?
- Confide in those you trust that you're ready to open up and start dating. Ask for accountability and support if that will help you stay motivated.
- For now, focus on love confidence, not on meeting your forever partner. Embrace connection for connection's sake as you open up more.
- Learn the foundations of flirting (in the next chapter) and practice, practice, practice!

Mantra for the Avoider:

I open myself up to give and receive love more deeply than I ever thought possible.

The Looper Assignment

Be proud of yourself for being courageous enough to date in the face of some unpleasant experiences. There's nothing fundamentally wrong with you, but that doesn't mean you can't do dating better. You can! Shift your focus to how it feels to be with the people you're meeting. Don't project onto them qualities and availability they haven't yet consistently shown you. Make dating more about your relationship needs than being liked and chosen.

Tips for the Looper:

- Break the cycle by upending how you've been dating. Delete or overhaul your old dating profiles, be more proactive in who you want to date (rather than waiting to see who chooses you), and ditch your typical ways of meeting people. Go on different types of dates and see what starts to shift.
- Take stock of what you've already learned. At what point can you recognize your old pattern showing up? Recognizing and walking away from the wrong person sooner and/or choosing new actions will bring the change you're seeking.
- Focus on breaking old patterns, and practice tons of self-validation (and compassion, of course) along the way.
- Block out all the bad dating stories that are normalizing your circumstances. Not everyone is having the same bad experiences over and over. Get (compassionately) curious about how you can take more agency over how you date.

Mantra for the Looper:

My history is not my destiny. I have the power to break old patterns and attract a loving partner.

how to find true love

The Surfer Assignment

Your powers of attraction are stellar. But as you've learned by now, attraction alone doesn't make relationships last. As you know, it's really hard to walk away from a strong romantic attraction. To change that, your main assignment is to slow things down and start looking at your love interests more holistically. Don't rearrange your whole life to accommodate someone you've just met. Pay attention to character and any red flags that you normally overlook. See if they have the patience to proceed slowly and build trust without love bombing you. Notice your own tendencies to get carried away too quickly. Self-compassion and self-care will assist you greatly as you make new choices.

Tips for the Surfer:

- Chemistry does not equal compatibility! Don't take your mutual attraction as the sign to throw caution to the wind and ride the wave.
- There's no rush. This moment is not your one chance at love. If they're your person, they'll be your person a month from now. If they can't wait, then they were never your person. Patience is more than just a virtue; it's also a muscle. Flex yours with a lot of compassionate practice.
- Get clear on your relationship values and give yourself permission to compare how your new boo aligns with them or doesn't.
- Challenge yourself to experiment with sparking chemistry with someone more grounded and purposeful than your usual type.
- Don't worry, even when you start dating more balanced partners, you'll still be a pro at bringing the heat.

Mantra for the Surfer:
It is safe for me to give and receive lasting love with a compatible partner.

The Sailor Assignment

A word about Sailors: The dating confidence spectrum can sometimes be a circle. Sailors who've had long-term relationships back-to-back for many years can have difficulty knowing how to slow things down. They might also discover that their relationships, while committed, haven't been particularly satisfying. For these reasons, some Sailors run the risk of moving into an Avoider phase; in the absence of knowing how to change their pattern, they sometimes opt out of romance and retreat entirely. On the flip side, some single Sailors go the route of chasing excitement and chemistry to avoid commitment over fear of landing in the wrong relationship again.

Tips for the Sailor:

- If you've conflated "relationship-minded" with boring, you run the risk of overcorrecting by now choosing the most exciting, least relationship-minded matches you can find. Your past relationships might have been or gotten boring, but you're not boring! You can both be committed (if that's what you still want) and in a vibrant relationship.
- Take time on your own, and with friends and family. Take that class. Follow that intuition that it's time to do something just for you. Normalize pouring into yourself whether you're partnered or single.
- Maybe you've never really been single, or never took the time to think proactively about what you want in a relationship. Well, now's your time to do just that. You have more than enough lived experience to mine in order to figure out what your heart really desires.
- With the rapidly changing dating landscape, things might look radically different from the last time you dated. You might have a technical learning curve, but your Sailor abilities remain.

Mantra for the Sailor:
I can effortlessly attract the relationship of my dreams.

Tips for All Archetypes

- Write down a vision of the version of you who has the love you want. In what way(s) are they showing up/doing life differently than you have been up until now?
- What's one thing you will commit to doing right away to get you one step closer to the vision you've just described?

Heartwork

Visit www.francescahogi.com/resources to take the Dating Archetype quiz.

Once you have your archetype, reflect:

1. Does this archetype resonate with me? Why or why not?
2. Can I see how or if my archetype has changed over time? Has it changed in wanted or unwanted ways?
3. Given what I've learned about the archetypes, what resonates as my current dating assignment?

CHAPTER 13

connect through flirting

The desire for romantic love is fueled by the human need for deep connection and intimacy. Dating, as a practice, is all about the search for connection. Some are seeking connection for a night, a few intoxicating weeks, or a lifetime. Even the self-care concept of "dating oneself" as a means of discovering who you are and your own lovability is about connection. The concepts you've learned this far, such as centering love, are also about making the connection between all aspects of your life and the power of love.

We all want it, we all need it, and yet, modern dating is stymied by a fundamental challenge—the inability to meaningfully connect. Paradoxically, our hyper-connected digital world has come to dominate our real-life reality. We're not feeling lonely and disconnected because our Wi-Fi isn't fast enough or we don't have enough followers on social media. Human connection is the most natural thing in the world, and yet it's still a skill that needs to be nurtured to do it well. In a world where it's possible to live your entire life through a screen, with no face-to-face or skin-to-skin contact, it takes a concerted effort to connect more and more meaningfully, especially when it comes to dating.

The digital dating industry has successfully convinced millions around the world that you need an app to date. A common frustration I've heard since the proliferation of dating apps is "I want to go on more dates, but I hate dating apps." This immediately tells me two things are likely about this person: (1) They're uncomfortable with flirting or don't know how to flirt effectively (more on that later), and (2) they live life with romantic blinders on. I know this because those who embrace romantic possibility in their lives and feel comfortable putting romantic intention into action through flirting are not dependent on dating apps, though they might use them to supplement their IRL efforts.

Flirting Fosters Romantic Connection

Flirting is a superpower. It has many purposes, but foremost it's how we put our intention for romantic connection in action. It's not necessarily about sexual attraction or intent, as is often assumed. You can have sex without flirting (depressingly), and you can flirt without a promise of sex. When done correctly, flirting is an invitation to a moment of connection. That might practically look like a two-second smile or a sincere passing compliment. In another context, it might feel like someone leaning in close to whisper in your ear, or you placing a hand on their thigh.

Flirting is a flexible and adaptable practice. In some circumstances, there might not be any romantic attraction present, just a moment of shared energy with another person. In others, you might feel like you're being consumed by the electricity of physical chemistry. How amazing is it that we can experience pure magic when both ends of that connection stay open? That's human connection, and it's what we all need most of all.

When used in all its layers and permutations, flirting can serve a variety of purposes. It is the single most important dating and connecting skill there is. Misunderstood as it is, most people leave the power of flirting on the table, or use it *too* selectively, waiting for the rare occasion where instant chemistry happens.

What Flirting Is . . . and Isn't

What comes to mind when you think of flirting? The cultural programming is: being overtly sexual or teasing with someone you want to hook up with. "Being a flirt" is rarely meant as a compliment, but rather an indictment of being frivolous, manipulative, attention-seeking, and oversexed. In our sex-shaming culture, this message can create an invisible shadow blocking your receptivity to romantic attention.

You've already learned how much belief matters to your romantic life. If you see yourself as sinful or shameful in any way for flirting, it's time to rethink what you've been taught. There is absolutely nothing wrong with flirting for the sake of all the sexual frivolity your heart desires. If everyone is a consenting adult, I fully support you. However, since our goal here is to find true love, my call to expand your beliefs around flirting is more relevant to those dating for true love, not frivolity. To my flirting newbies, get excited! Your intention matters, and if your intention is to activate your romantic energy, you've already begun.

Normalizing Flirting

On the flip side of flirting shame, many men have told me that they fear appearing predatory or aggressive if they flirt with someone who hasn't already expressed interest in them. Some queer, trans, or gender nonconforming people have the very valid concern of how their efforts might be received by others who are bigoted or simply not interested in dating people of their identity. And just about everyone knows the fear of rejection that can be triggered by even the smallest display of vulnerability.

So what happens when people grow too afraid to flirt or uncomfortable being flirted with? You have a whole bunch of amazing single people wanting romantic connection but blocking it with their limiting beliefs around their ability to connect. By choosing flirting as a way to strengthen your human connection muscle, you move it beyond the romantic and into the zone of your commitment to centering love.

You and I can help to normalize flirting (and maybe change the world) by redefining it in a more holistic way:

Words and/or actions done with the intention of making another person feel seen, special, and acknowledged.

Underneath the stories we've been told about flirting is this foundational, almost neutral understanding of what sparks, builds, and maintains connection. What makes us feel more loved, more human, than being seen and valued? Imagine a world where that was a choice more people make—or even every single person makes. That is a world I want to live in.

The Problems Flirting Solves

Flirting solves many of dating's biggest obstacles, and even many of the challenges in maintaining romantic connection over time. Flirting's importance is probably obvious for the dating phase of your journey, but perhaps less so for what happens after the relationship is formed. No matter how much attraction might be present in the early, or honeymoon, phase, if you take that chemistry for granted, it will decrease over time. Intimacy and connection isn't "set it and forget it"—it requires intention and nurturing. "The spark is gone" is a common reason that relationships end. If you're only focused on flirting to get into the relationship, but then cease making effort to maintain that energy, your relationship will reflect that lack of effort. Bottom line is: When you get better at flirting, you not only make your meeting and courtship process smoother, but you also increase your chances of making romantic connection last over time.

Dormant romantic energy: Always being seen platonically, only approached romantically by people who are either clueless or see you as a challenge. This situation can feel especially frustrating and deepen fears around rejection or never finding a great partner.

Difficulty reading romantic cues: If it only dawns on you the next day or six months later that the cute guy with the blue hat at the party was flirting with you, or not at all until someone else points out your admirer, I'm talking to you.

Being dating app dependent/inability to meet matches IRL: It's typically fear that keeps people from finding real-world connection. Fear of being rejected, of sending the wrong message, of not being someone's type, of a culture where most people are heads down in their phones... Who cares that most people are always looking at their phones? You don't have to be one of them. Be the change you want to see in the world and make eye contact!

Only attracting people who see you as a challenge: A discomfort with flirting is a sign of romantic insecurity, and that makes you a target for people who don't respect your boundaries. In the highly toxic and unethical "pickup artist" community, men learn strategies to sexually "conquer" women. One of their primary tactics is to find a woman who looks uncomfortable receiving attention and manipulate her insecurities. Having a comfort level with flirting makes women in particular a less appealing target of this type of predatory behavior.

Being more susceptible to love bombing (non-malicious as well as intentionally manipulative): On the extreme end of the love bombing spectrum are prolific scammers causing immeasurable emotional and financial harm daily online. Just as get-rich-quick schemes seek people desperate for cash, romance schemes are seeking those desperate for romance. Therefore, by watering your own romantic garden, you're less thirsty and tempted when someone disingenuous comes along.

Overreliance on instant chemistry (especially when you're breaking a pattern): As we covered in chapter 6, instant chemistry is often an unreliable indicator of long-term compatibility. In fact, if you have a strong pattern you're in the process of breaking, it's at least a yellow flag, if not an outright red one. When you empower yourself to flirt with the intention of exploring or sparking chemistry in a healthier dynamic, you begin redirecting your chemistry radar.

Potentially missing out on great matches by prematurely jumping to conclusions: You've been taught your whole life to chase the spark of instant chemistry. It's time to try your energetic hand at becoming a conscious co-creator of chemistry, not just an unconscious one. As Dr. Maya Angelou said—when you know better, you do better.

Not being able to capitalize on the moments you do have a flash of connection or chemistry: Have you ever kicked yourself for not taking advantage of a passing moment of connection? Develop your own flirting mojo and never feel at a loss in a critical moment again.

Inability to keep chemistry going over time: Your relationship won't be sexy (or stay sexy for long) if you and your partner don't have the skill of making one another feel seen, special, acknowledged, desirable, and desired.

Low love confidence: The more romantically activated you become, the more you see and experience romantic potential.

Disconnection from the fun and energy of romance: Romantically activate yourself through your self-love, intention-setting, and flirting practices, and discover your unique mojo.

Fears of rejection: It's true, they might not be interested. Also, they might be by the time you effectively connect with them. This isn't about wearing someone down or winning them over; it's an awareness that sometimes you have the chance to spark chemistry. Even if you don't, know you'll be okay.[1]

The Purposes of Flirting

When I talk to singles about flirting, they sometimes have a knee-jerk reaction, saying, "I don't want to give someone the wrong impression," or "There's no one I'm interested in flirting with." If you can relate to that response, take heart. There is more than one reason to flirt, and different styles of flirting have different appropriateness given your circumstances:

Exploring/potentially sparking chemistry: So many people hold themselves back from doing this, especially if they've been conditioned to make snap judgments like you're swiping on an app. Chemistry is about more than just looks, so if you really want to find the right next person for you, give yourself the chance to tap into the energy of who you're meeting and allow yourself to be surprised by who you connect with.

Making someone's day: If you succeed in making someone feel seen, special, and acknowledged, the worst that can happen is you make their day brighter. The less attached you are to the outcome, the more you'll give this gift to others.

Conveying desirability: The most commonly acknowledged purpose of flirting is this one—let someone know you want them. There are plenty of ways to achieve this! Desirability is another layer to

---

1 Depending on your gender and sexual orientation, there is an added layer of personal safety to take into account. LGBTQIA people are more at risk for violence or unpleasant reactions. Women who date men are more at risk of any positive attention being taken as a sexual come-on. My advice still applies—but I'd be remiss if I didn't acknowledge there's another element of personal safety to be aware of. Make sure you are in a safe environment and read the body language and social cues of the people you're interacting with. If your intuition is sending alarms—please listen.

flirting's foundation of making someone feel seen and special. Experiment with what feels good and appropriate for the circumstances.

Getting in a meet-cute mindset: The biggest objection I hear to adopting an MCM is a lack of prospects; when you normalize flirting, you start seeing more evidence of romantic possibility everywhere you go.

One bold move: Sometimes you've got to swing for the fences. Your gut tells you to connect with this person; they are just too adorable to pass by. Met briefly in person, but don't know if they're interested or available? Ask a mutual friend for an introduction or follow up with a DM on social media (it works, I've done it).

The Building Blocks of Effective Flirting

Soon we'll dive into the different styles of flirting and in which contexts they work best. But first, let's review the building blocks of effective flirting.

Intention: As discussed, the benefit of intention is twofold—it activates you energetically to align with that intention emotionally and mentally, and it activates the power of universal intention (love), boosting your efforts. Ask yourself, *What do I want to achieve in this encounter?*

Eye contact: It feels intimate because it is. Eye contact breaks through a shield that keeps others at a distance. No staring contests necessary, nor is looking everyone in the eye everywhere you go. However, a comfort (or willingness to develop more comfort) with the vulnerability required will take you to the next level of connecting. Practice makes prepared, and I recommend practicing more eye contact now. Don't wait until you see someone you're interested in to try this out; normalize it as your way of moving through the world.

Presence: If someone was "flirting" with you but looking at their phone screen every ten seconds, it's unlikely you'd feel very seen, special, or acknowledged. Whether it's outer distraction or a running commentary in your head that keeps you from being in the moment, set yourself up to win. Minimize the physical distractions that come from technology, especially those little computers in our pockets and purses. Use deep breathing to help calm your thoughts and bring you out of your head and into your body.

Enthusiasm: We're unlikely to convey an intention of connection without demonstrating some enthusiasm for whoever we're engaging with. Don't play it so cool that you lose your chance to spark some heat.

Body language: You don't have to be an expert in body language to notice when someone feels more closed off/unapproachable versus relaxed and open. If I asked you to describe how someone might sit on a subway train or at a party who did *not* want to be approached versus someone who did, you probably wouldn't describe the same body language. Notice your own body language when you find yourself in these moments of potential connection. Do you tense up, or are you more at ease? Do you lean in, or do you cross your arms and legs? Using your intention, breath, and awareness, begin to feel yourself into a more inviting posture.

Energy/vibe: All of these factors combine to form your energy around interacting with others. You know how some people exude magnetism and charisma, and others hostility or caution? Some people's energy is so strong you can't help but consciously notice it. That's not the only energetic read you're picking up on—and just as you're sensing those around you, they're sensing you as well.

When you are clear and comfortable with these elements, your natural flirting style will flourish, and your romantic flow along with it.

The Eight Flirting Styles

There are different ways to flirt, and they have varying levels of effectiveness given the context and the comfort level of those involved. Here are eight different styles I've identified to get you started in increasing your own flirting know-how and adaptability.

#1: Attentiveness

Ever meet someone new and notice they're giving you their full attention with real fascination? They not only ask you questions but also seem genuinely interested in your answers? (Unlike a lot of "small talk" banter, which can feel empty and perfunctory.) How about feeling yourself more drawn or endeared to them *because* of their attention? Such is the power of attentiveness in helping us to feel seen, special, and acknowledged for who we are.

Attentiveness tip: If you're good at being attentive but not at conveying anything more than platonic or professional interest, push yourself to experiment with bringing some more vulnerability and intention to your interactions. Don't talk about work, for instance, if that's a default comfort zone for you. Be bold and notice your body language signals.

Energy of attentiveness: *I find you so fascinating! Tell me more.*

#2: Complimentary

The power of a sincere compliment in sparking a nice moment of connection can't be overstated. Just putting a smile on someone's face is its own reward, and I encourage you to embrace that intention. One of my favorite heartwork assignments for clients is to challenge them to give compliments to passing strangers, with no attachment to the outcome. Particularly when you're encountering someone in passing, a compliment can be a great way to make a meet-cute moment of your very own.

Complimentary tip: Be more imaginative than "you're hot" type statements (if you're looking for something more involved than a hookup, that is). Commenting on someone's style, the way they creatively place their coffee order, or their cool shoes are all simple examples. Be creative—and most of all, be sincere.

Energy of complimentary: *I like what I see/experience with you.*

#3: Formal

I can't say I "recommend" this style per se, but it definitely works for the right people. The best way to describe formality is as "traditional" or even "old-fashioned." This is the territory of chivalry—opening doors, pulling out chairs, a kiss on the hand, and communicating in a very polite and formal way. Think *Bridgerton* or a dozen roses with a card that reads "Would you do me the honor of having dinner with me?" Could be sweet, right? Not the everyday way of flirting in our modern times, and in my experience, it can often come across as performative or rigid. For that reason, I don't recommend it unless—and this is an important distinction—it's aligned with your personality and it's a courtship tradition your love interest appreciates.

Energy of formal: *I'm performing a ritual of courtship because I'm romantically interested in you.*

#4: Playful/Teasing

I generally consider this a more "advanced" flirting style because success at it requires nuance and a good ability to pick up on energy and social cues. Sometimes people think they're flirting by teasing, but it can translate as being rude, clueless, or even negging (intentionally putting someone down to trigger their insecurities). However, cheeky body language (winking, the classic hair toss, etc.) can be very effective at providing the invitation needed to spark a connection.

Playful/teasing tip: If it's your personality to engage in witty banter and you know when it's being well-received, then go for it!

Otherwise, focus on the preceding foundations and practice reading the "vibe" to hone your skill.

Energy of playful: *I enjoy provoking a playful reaction from you.*

#5: Saying Something

If you see someone, say something. My matchmaking BFF, Amy Van Doran, has a great saying when it comes to maximizing your chances of meeting someone organically. "Better you say something than nothing at all." In this spirit, I'm including the catch-all style of "saying something." All that's required is seizing an opportunity to connect with someone interesting or intriguing and being a bit brave. Maybe it's a question, a comment about something going on around you, the food they just ordered, or even a (respectful) DM slide. Even if it's awkward, your opening line might be something you'll laugh about together for years to come.

Energy of saying something: *I'm all in on making this moment of connection happen.*

#6: Physical Touch

Purposes: Making someone's day, sparking romantic connection when not instantaneous, feeling more connected generally, strengthening your mojo, making the world a better place, testing the waters of someone's interest/availability.

When flirting is the intention, a wide range of touch can fall under this umbrella. This can be an "advanced" move or a relatively benign one.

Context matters here. Physical touch might be welcome or appropriate, or it might be too soon or triggering. In general, however, once you're touching someone, you're escalating the encounter. In the context of an ongoing relationship, you and your partner have the chance to learn each other's preferences around physical intimacy. When you're at the beginning of meeting or getting to know someone, pay close attention to the body language of anyone you're touching, and err on the side of asking for consent for anything more than a handshake. You never know how any one person might be triggered by touch, especially by a stranger. Proceed with respect and awareness.

Physical Touch tip: There is a wide cultural range for what is considered appropriate or offensive when it comes to physical touch. Women in particular all too often experience unwanted touch, so be mindful of presumptuously crossing any boundaries.

Energy of Physical Touch: *I want to be physically closer to you.*

#7: Overt/Bold

If you, like me, are a fan of the iconic television show *The Golden Girls*, you surely remember the many exploits of the sexually uninhibited character of Blanche Devereaux. A central feature of Blanche's personality and topic of many of the show's best jokes was her unabashed ability to hit on men in the most direct and shameless (in a good way—without shame) way possible. No matter where she went, if she saw an "eligible" man, she was sure to let him know her interest in and availability for romance and, often, sex.

This type of flirting is excellent when you have already established a romantic, and especially a physical, connection with someone. However, respecting other people's boundaries should always be taken into consideration. It is very easy to trigger or offend someone you don't have an established rapport with when using this style. For women in particular, this approach can be unwelcome and can make them feel unsafe.

Be mindful if the energy between you is conducive to this approach, and err on the side of caution when using it. Even when your overt behavior is welcome, when used as an opening line to a stranger, it's less effective unless you're looking for (as Blanche often was) a short-term "good time."

Overt/Bold tip: You might try on the boldness without the sexual element (e.g., making a strong effort to get someone's attention, crossing a crowded room to speak to someone sitting at a table with a group of friends, or sending over a drink—Blanche would surely approve).

Overt/Bold energy: *I see something in you I like, and I want you to know it.*

#8: Coy/Enticing

Some people boldly walk across the room to introduce themselves to a stranger, and others invite that level of boldness. This is a very effective flirting style when you have comfort with eye contact, playfulness, and receiving romantic attention. Anyone can and should practice this style, but if you've never flirted with anyone before, it might freak you out too much. Ideally you'd employ your enticement tactics when you're someplace you'll be for a little while, and you have more than one chance to send nonverbal cues (e.g., smiling, repeated eye contact) to convey your openness.

Coy/Enticing tip: If you've heard you give off "unapproachable" vibes, then I encourage you to practice drawing people to you. How you feel matters, so be your own cheerleader or practice with a trusted wing person.

Coy/Enticing energy: *Come closer, I won't bite.*

Effective Flirting

To effectively harness the power of flirting, understanding what works best when is key. How you would flirt with a stranger in line at the coffee shop vs. how you would flirt with an intimate partner will (and at times should) be different. For our purposes, I've grouped flirting into two levels, with recommended flirting styles for each.

Level 1: Foundational flirting—words and/or actions done with the intention of making another person feel seen, special, acknowledged.

Level 1 flirting styles:

- Attentive
- Complimentary
- Formal
- Playful/teasing
- Coy/enticing

Additional Level 1 actions:

- Striking up a conversation (anything from introducing yourself to asking how the book is they're reading)
- Moving yourself into physical proximity (e.g., breaking away from your group of friends to stand near them at the bar)
- Nonverbal cues like the classic "hair toss" or smiling at them

Level 2: Words and/or actions done with the intention of making another person feel seen, special, acknowledged, AND desirable OR desired by you specifically.

Level 2 flirting styles:

- Even more attentive
- Even more complimentary
- Formal (if it resonates with your love interest)
- Even more playful/teasing
- Even more coy/enticing
- Physical touch
- Overt/bold

Additional Level 2 actions:

- Sending over a drink or dessert in a restaurant
- Passing someone your phone number
- Sliding into someone's DMs or sending them a note

No matter the context or your intention, always remember to honor boundaries and to pay attention to how your efforts are being received. Romantic interest is no excuse for being overly familiar or aggressive, or to intrude on someone's personal space. Shoot your shot, but don't become entitled for the reaction you want. Err on the side of respectful caution.

Heartwork

Remember self-compassionate curiosity and that you don't have to do anything perfectly. That includes flirting. Practice makes prepared, and that's what I challenge you to do.

- Practice "gentle" eye contact with as many people as you can. Notice what comes up for you and breathe through any discomfort. It's not a staring contest, so you don't need to hold prolonged eye contact for this to be a valuable exercise. Also pay attention to when eye contact is not comfortable for someone else. Don't take it personally, but respect their body language and look away.
- Practice increased vulnerability with friends and family. Communicate how you're really feeling.

Share that you're embarking on a new phase of your love journey and you'd love their support.*

- Observe what step(s) you can take to reduce or eliminate the things that make connecting with others more challenging (e.g., a habit of always being on your phone, negative self-talk, etc.).
- Visualize the most magnetic version of you and channel that energy to guide and inspire you.
- TALK TO STRANGERS! Don't wait until you see someone you're attracted to or where you see romantic potential. The world is a better place for your efforts to engage with your fellow humans. Plus, you never know what serendipity it might lead to.
- Practice breathing when you feel triggered/afraid/ unsure. Taking new action to let others into your energetic space can feel really uncomfortable or cause you to shut down. Be gentle with yourself (again, be mindful of your self-talk—keep it kind and encouraging) and practice deep breathing to help soothe your nervous system.

*I recommend the book *Daring Greatly* by Brené Brown for a deep dive on vulnerability and how to powerfully reframe and increase your comfort with it.

CHAPTER 14

bring the love to dating

Is love your priority? Are you answering your heart's call for more of it? Or is fear or avoidance what consumes most of your romantic energy? We can all see how deeply fear is embedded in dating culture. Your intention to rise above that fear transforms how you date. When working with new clients, the first thing we do together is set goals. Rather than focusing on what's wrong, we start with *what do you want?* If the answer is true love, then how you date should reflect that.

If you are committed to love, then the experience of dating you should look and feel different than dating someone who isn't. When someone tells me they want true love, but their behavior is indistinguishable from someone looking for casual hookups, that's evidence of a major disconnect. If, for example, on a dating app you're posting sexy photos and a generic bio designed to get as many matches as possible, what about that approach reflects your desire to get the *right* matches? Or if you're playing dating games like waiting a certain number of days to reply to a message, or trying to make someone jealous, where is the love in that?

The path to true love is one powered by intention. Your sincere intention manifests as an inner commitment to love. Once you make that commitment, your outer behavior will change as a result.

Date Differently

Any fears you have associated with dating, as we've already covered, are not your fault. What comes next, however, is your responsibility. You already know that dating from fear is the hard way. Your next step is to commit to dating with more ease.

Given the courtship methods society has dreamed up, dating has the greatest potential for forming true love relationships today—but not as it's currently practiced by most people. Why? Beyond the issues of fear and worthiness exists a fundamental misunderstanding people have about dating and relationships. That's the belief that it's all supposed to be effortless. You're supposed to look at someone and know in that instant they're your forever soulmate (or not). You're supposed to have a line of suitors out the door, all vying for your affection. In truth, it takes effort to be loving. It takes effort to transcend the chaos and bring the love to modern dating. What dating from love looks like for you is what we'll explore in this chapter, and what I challenge you to reflect on in your own heart.

Date with Intention

"Just put yourself out there" is one of the most annoying pieces of dating advice in history. Because what does that even mean? Hopefully by now, you're clearer on what that answer is for you. Dating is not one-size-fits-all, and factors like your dating archetype provide big clues as to what's best for you at any given time. In my course How to Date with Intention, I walk students through an entire pre-dating process to get clear on what they hope to get out of this adventure that is dating.

As we covered in chapter 10, intention—like joy, creativity, and love—is infinite. You don't have to "create" intention; just tap into it, letting its insights, serendipities, and blessings show you the path forward. Such is the power of romantic flow. When you bring intention to dating (and all else you do when you care about the outcome), you manifest guidance as to what Oprah Winfrey calls "your next best step." That next step is often the only thing we can see, and even when we can't, we can still set an intention to do so.

We don't manifest and keep love or anything else without doing our part to be the version of us who inevitably has that thing. Intention is the path to reveal that version of us more clearly, like an archaeologist chipping away at an ancient fresco.

In dating, you can use the power of intention on the micro level by asking, "What's my intention for this date?" Here's a sampling of some client dating intentions:

- *To see if I can feel comfortable with a stranger*
- *To practice flirting*
- *To find out something interesting about my date*
- *To share something I normally wouldn't*
- *To stay sober*
- *To focus on being present in my body*
- *To see if I like them and want to see them again*

What these have in common is their location in "your" department. Whereas an intention to "meet the love of my life tonight" wouldn't be.

For a macro view of your current intentions as you embark on a new season of dating, here are some questions to ask yourself:

1. **Why am I dating?** Start with the end you want in mind.
2. **What kind of experience do I want to have?** For example, *I want to explore my fun and spontaneous side with emotionally safe partners.*
3. **What can I do to positively contribute to that outcome?** For example, *By choosing people to date who are both emotionally grounded and sparkling with good energy.*

Prioritize Character

As Dr. Maya Angelou said: "When someone shows you who they are, believe them the first time." Dating from love starts with self-love. It is self-loving to partner with people who are trustworthy and have integrity. Extending grace or projecting best intentions on another person shouldn't come at the expense of honoring yourself. All relationships will have highs and lows. None of us are perfect. But ask yourself—who will follow through? Who's consistent in their words and actions? Who has the character I'm seeking in a true love partner?

"I really like this new guy and he's so sweet to me. But the mean things he says about other people are concerning. I don't want to be too picky or judge him, though." A client shared her observation of this disconnect with some uncertainty. "Would you be friends with someone who spoke about others like that?" I asked her. "No! I'd be so embarrassed if any of my friends heard some of the things he says."

If someone doesn't meet your standard for friendship, why would you want to date them? Sincerely ask yourself that question. Only in a world where we've been brainwashed into thinking romance overrides everything else would we assume character doesn't matter, only attraction does. Would you consider not wanting friends with misaligned values as being judgmental? Probably not. Dating from love doesn't mean making yourself a martyr to someone's poor behavior. It means loving yourself to a high enough standard that you're only moving forward with those who meet that standard. When you see cracks in the façade of how someone is presenting themselves to you, pay attention.

Lastly, don't forget that dating is a two-way street. Are you holding yourself to a standard of strong character and honest communication? Are you showing up in a way that lets your potential partner(s) know that you can be trusted and relied upon? Just as you need a safe place for your heart in order to keep it open, the people you're in relationships with need the same.

Know Your Dealbreakers

What are your absolute dealbreakers? These aren't preferences like "I hate that dumb haircut" or "They don't like sci-fi"—if you are really crazy about someone, their hair is unlikely to be the reason you don't proceed. Dealbreakers are the traits or behaviors that are a *hard no* for you, even if all else was aligned—for example, lying, substance abuse, bigotry, conflicting religious beliefs, refusal to/insistence on a prenuptial agreement, etc. One note about dealbreakers—no need to broadcast them to the world. Don't list them in your dating app profile or announce them on social media. Focus on what you want, not what you don't. Once you're clear on what your *hard nos* are, you can move on. That's how you move forward on your journey—by being more committed to love than anything else.

Use Dating Apps as a Tool

I haven't had many good things to say about how technology has impacted dating and therefore relationship culture. However, people can and do still meet great partners online. Most people are terrible at the apps or using social media for dating because of their superficial approach. They also tend to overestimate their ability to decide who they'd actually like in real life.

Here are a few guidelines to use dating apps in a better way:

Speak to who you want to meet: Most profiles are generic and geared toward getting as many matches as possible. Instead, try putting yourself in the shoes of the kinds of people you want to meet and speak directly to them.

Don't swipe into the void: Apps create what social psychologist Barry Schwartz termed "the paradox of choice." His work suggests having more options paradoxically makes it harder to choose and leaves us feeling less satisfied with our choices. Don't fall into the trap of thinking you can just keep swiping until you find someone perfect.

Delete your old profile: If you've been on an app for more than six months, especially if you haven't been using it regularly, delete it and start over. Your old profile is an algorithmic no-person's land, unlikely to be seen by anyone other than your fellow inconsistent daters.

Don't be so hasty: Slow down. Read profiles before you match with someone. Don't just choose the hottest or most appealing profiles you can find. They might not even be real people. Rather than ask, *Is this someone I can see myself with?* based on a few pics and a tiny bio, ask: *Is this someone I can see myself talking to for ten minutes?* Plenty of profiles won't meet that standard, but it's a more effective and realistic strategy.

Most importantly, be sure that you're using any apps as a supplement to your real-life efforts to show up ready for romantic connection.

Your Dating Self-Care Plan

In chapter 4 we talked about self-care as a 3-part question: First, *How do I want to feel?* Second, *Am I doing anything that conflicts with how I want to feel?* Lastly, *What action(s) can I take to contribute to that outcome?* Reflect on these questions as they specifically apply to how you date. Dating self-care is the way you practically support maintaining your commitment to love. The foundation of that commitment is of course your own relationship with you. There are many hallmarks of self-loving action in dating: healthy boundaries, resting, listening to your gut, saying no to what you don't want, etc. Use self-love as a verb and you'll improve dating and everything else.

You might consider:

- timing—when you date, where, and what arrangements you might need to facilitate;
- how to turn someone down gracefully (e.g., "It's been nice getting to know you, but I don't think we're a match");
- what kinds of dating activities/locations would be fun, comfortable, or interesting to you.

Dating is serious business that can and should be enjoyable. Protecting your energy and balancing openness with boundaries is its own spiritual practice. For that reason, knowing how best to set yourself up to thrive while dating is a good idea.

Dating self-care to consider:

- **Journaling:** Writing down your thoughts and experiences can help you process your feelings and ground yourself in the perspective of lessons learned along your love journey.
- **Voice-noting:** Like journaling, but spoken out loud and recorded.

- **Regular movement:** Moving your body boosts your mood and energy.
- **Prioritize social connection:** Hang out with your friends. Call your family members. Be an engaged community member. Investing in your overall "social health," as author and researcher Kasley Killam describes in her book *The Art and Science of Connection*[1], has mental, physical, and emotional benefits.

Green Flags

It can be easy to focus on what's wrong with others (or yourself) and to develop a vigilance about "red flags" in dating. Again, clarity on what's a no for you, in terms of how people treat you and the presence of dealbreakers, is liberating. You don't have to walk around constantly reminding yourself not to do things you're unlikely to do (e.g., Note to self: "Don't throw myself on the ground and throw a tantrum in the airport today"). Same goes for reminding yourself not to date people who have anger issues or treat you with indifference.

Instead of what you don't want, it's time to seek out what you do. Here are some examples of dating green flags to observe in others and display yourself:

- Demonstrates respect and kindness toward all
- Consistency in words and actions
- Proactively communicating and making effort to move things forward
- Clear and respectful communication
- Enthusiasm for dating you and getting to know your authentic self

---

1 Kasley Killam, *The Art and Science of Connection: Why Social Health Is the Missing Key to Living Longer, Healthier, and Happier* (HarperOne, 2024).

- Patience to proceed without love bombing
- Personal accountability
- Ability to define and articulate love goals
- Self-love

Date RAW

RAW is a guideline to follow when you're looking for a significant relationship. Ready, able, and willing—all three are ideally present within both you and your love interest. When only one or two of these elements is present, it can lead to an extremely confusing relationship. RAW dating will save you precious time and provide more safety for your precious heart and those you date. It's also a path to more self-understanding about how you show up in dating.

1. **Ready:** *I am ready for a relationship.*

I have coached more people than I can count through heartbreak after a relationship ends where this basic common-ground understanding was never established. Being able to articulate what you are seeking romantically is the baseline of higher-level dating. If you wanted to buy a house, wouldn't you establish the house was for sale before you started touring it and measuring it for drapes? Asking if the house is for sale doesn't mean you've decided to buy the house, and it doesn't guarantee your offer would be accepted even if you did. It simply means it's a basic possibility you might choose to explore.

Just as your inner love program is always guiding your romantic decisions, the same goes for everyone else. Another person's readiness for a relationship is *independent* of you. Someone can be head over heels in love with you and still not be ready to commit. (That's the confusion I want you to avoid.) Discussing this upfront is asking,

"What kind of relationship are you ready for at this point in your life?" Not "Do you want to be with me forever?"

Some people who are less evolved on their love journey than you might attempt to shame or gaslight you into thinking you have no right to ask this question, or that by asking you'll scare off a potential match. If someone doesn't have the maturity to know the difference between "Is the house for sale?" and "Will you please sell me your house?" I would argue they're doing you a favor by taking themselves out of the equation. Don't worry—the wrong people leaving make space for the right ones to arrive.

Your new boo saying, "Yes, I'm totally ready for a forever relationship" doesn't guarantee it's true, that they're capable of receiving love, or that the two of you will wind up together. It's simply the first step in determining if it's worth exploring if you're a good fit. In my experience, an inability to articulate readiness is typically a sign that they're not. Same goes for you. Are you ready to say what you are seeking romantically?

2. **Able: *I am able to co-create the kind of relationship we both want.***

Assessing readiness can start with a simple question. Not so with "able," which is best observed over time. You can think of it as the capacity to let yourself have and hold the love you want. Like readiness, however, inner capacity for a healthy partnership is independent of the other person. If you run away from everyone who loves you, that pattern doesn't end until you're ready to change it. Same goes for those you date—how they show up for you is mostly a reflection of where their ability lies.

Here are some questions for reflection on the question of able:

- Do I feel seen and appreciated for who I am?
- How consistently am I/are they showing up?

- Do both of our words match our actions?
- Are there any red flags I'm overlooking?
- Are there any green flags I'm overlooking?
- Do I feel respected and safe? Do they?
- If this dynamic between us continued to strengthen, would it align with my highest good and vision of the love I want?

3. **Willing:** *I am willing to put in the effort to move things forward with you.*

Willing is the easiest of RAW to observe. Are they into you and able to show it? Is it pulling teeth to communicate with them or plan a date? Are they the ones who make all the effort and you passively go along for the ride, or vice versa? Mutual willingness to move a connection forward, deepening it as you go, is the ideal when *ready* and *able* are also present. Confusion and hurt feelings are the result when you're aligned on willing but not the rest.

"Why did they act like my boyfriend if they knew they weren't going to be?" A common scenario is to interpret willingness as readiness. We've discussed this before, but it bears repeating because it happens a lot. Peter's profile on a dating app says he's looking for a long-term relationship. Knowing that Taylor has seen his profile, he assumes they have the same goal; no conversation necessary. When Taylor is excited about spending time together, Peter again assumes they're on the same page. All is fine until things come to a head—by now Peter's and Taylor's feelings are strong, and Peter has finally brought up commitment only to be shocked by Taylor's lack of agreement. It's a tale as old as time, or at least as old as Tinder. Make assumptions in dating at your peril. They are the cause of many avoidable hurt feelings and lingering bitterness.

No Bad Dates

The story goes something like this: I had the worst date ever. We matched on a dating app on Tuesday night. We message back and forth all week (though I'm the one asking all the questions), and I suggest we meet up for drinks on Friday. They say they have dinner plans, but they can meet at X location at 5 p.m. I know that getting there on time from work is going to be stressful, but I really want to meet them! This is the furthest I've gotten in dating in months. Besides, they're busy later and if it doesn't happen now, it probably never will.

So I rush to get to X location at 5 p.m. I am sweaty and flustered and rush into the bathroom to pull myself together when I arrive. That's when I check my phone and see that they're running thirty minutes late! I am so annoyed (mostly at myself) but relieved the date is still happening. When they finally show up thirty-four minutes later, they immediately announce they only have "twenty-ish" minutes before they need to leave for dinner. No apology, no explanation, no *How can I make it up to you?* I tell myself: *You're here. Make the most of this.* They're actually really hot in person. And so I try to make conversation. They're not interested. They left before the check came, saying, "Venmo request me." And to make things worse, they unmatched me on the app and I didn't even have their phone number for the Venmo request that I was never going to make. What an asshole. I'm never dating again.

On so many levels, this hypothetical (but highly plausible) dating debacle was avoidable. From the pulling teeth to the location choice, to "hanging in there" because they're so eager to meet someone . . . there were no green flags present. I teach No Bad Dates (NBD) to avoid ever putting yourself in such a bad position. As you know by now, I am a fan of dating. It's an important process and one that teaches you so much about yourself, about connection, romance, and what love looks and feels like. Most of what we would call "bad" dates can be avoided with a simple, intentional dating strategy.

No Bad Dates isn't about avoiding all discomfort in dating and making every date amazing. When you're interacting with other humans, there's always a degree of unpredictability. NBD can help you avoid some of the foreseeable dating pitfalls. Your relationship is forming from the moment you connect—how you date matters. How does someone behave when they are present, enthusiastic, and sincerely interested in you? They don't waltz out of your micro-date saying, "Venmo me," I can tell you that much.

Here are the five pillars of NBD:

1. **Date selection:** Who you choose to go out with in the first place matters. Particularly when you're going on a first date with someone you've never met in person, pay attention to their behavior before you meet. If your communication feels off (inconsistencies or rudeness), they're demonstrating selfishness (let's have our first date at a bar on my corner, never mind it's an hour away from you), or pressuring you (just ditch your friends and come meet me) and other red flag behavior, do yourself a favor and pay attention.

2. **Date expectation:** Revisit your intentions for dating right now. Additionally, check in with what you'll consider a successful date. Can you reset any outsized pessimism (this is going to suck, like they always do) or overblown optimism (I know we haven't met yet, but they're so perfect) to a more neutral compromise?

3. **Date planning:** If you're a planner, plan. If you're not a planner, be spontaneous. Either way, communicate with your people. "Tonight I can't, but can we plan for this weekend? I'm available all day Saturday."

4. **Dating logistics:** If you hate dive bars and drinking, going on a date to a dive bar probably won't be your favorite. If squeezing in dates after work during the week stresses you out, commit to weekend dates. How you feel always matters and effective communication is key in relationships. You have the option to suggest something that feels more aligned with your personality and love goals. "Do you like photography? I've been wanting to see an exhibit uptown—want to check it out together?"

5. **Dating intuition:** "I had a feeling something was off when they made a rude comment about their ex. But I told myself I was being too judgmental." The importance of listening to your intuition while dating can't be said enough. Here's your reminder that your inner wisdom has invaluable guidance on the subject of your romantic life.

Yes, You Can Get a Date

I want to acknowledge that all this dating guidance can come off as beside the point if you don't date. Your experience might be of difficulty finding dates who meet your criteria, or finding dates at all. You might read all the unhelpful dating statistics about your demographic and how impossible it will be for you to find a suitable partner in this day and age. Let me tell you—there are people who would love to date you. You'll want to date some (but not all) of them too. If you're being honest with yourself, can you acknowledge some romantic possibility you've overlooked? Perhaps you suspect something you've been prioritizing in dating might not be as relevant as you'd previously believed?

There was a time when I didn't know how to get a date. It felt like I was living with an invisibility cloak that blocked me from romantic possibility. In terms of romantic flow, I didn't experience it until I was a frustrated young lawyer. My personal breakthrough started with a thought: *Well, I can't be the most undatable person in the world.* The possibility inspired me to start dating. I signed up for an online site (this was pre–dating apps) and I started sending messages. My goal was literally *learn how to date.* It wasn't to meet my forever person, or even to get into a relationship. My first milestone was going on a few dates, proving to myself there are people in this world I can romantically connect with. After a while, I noticed I wasn't getting asked on second dates. Since I'd already gone from zero dates to a few, I believed I could keep going and get to a second. And so that became my next milestone. Steadily, I saw that as my confidence and skill improved, so did my universe of romantic possibility.

Embrace dating as an experiment. Return to your awareness of the abundance of love in the universe. Be bold. Be willing to date against type. Release the stories of who definitely will or won't be interested in you. Allow yourself to be surprised.

Imagine I'm an eccentric billionaire who uses my money for good. In this hypothetical, I promise you one million dollars for each date you go on in the next thirty days with someone who meets your basic criteria (e.g., respectful and kind, *not* super-hot and rich). How many millions are you getting? In my experience asking this and similar questions, even the most demoralized dater perks up. No one says "none." Ideas start sparking, as well as a newly imagined boldness to approach multiple strangers daily and directly ask them out. If you, too, can imagine you'd find a way to make at least one date happen, then you've already shown yourself it's possible. Step into that sense of limitless possibility and see what happens next.

I know you can do it. Hopefully by now you've planted your flag on the side of love. Let it inspire and guide you.

Heartwork

Reflect on the following:

1. Do I have any resistance to communicating the type of relationship I'm ready for? Has the fear of how that honesty might be received held me back in the past?
2. Do I have any resistance to asking others what they're looking for? Why or why not?
3. Am I clear on what readiness looks like in action, or do I take words at face value? How can I get better at showing up with readiness in how I date and discerning other people's ability to be the partner I'm seeking?
4. Have I emotionally invested in people who didn't meet the RAW criteria? Have I been that person? How has that turned out in the past and how might it change my dating outcomes in the future?
5. How might No Bad Dates have helped me in the past? How might it help me going forward?

CHAPTER 15

find true love

If romantic love is a treasure hunt—it's a quest to find oneself. You are both the treasure and the adventurer in the process of building relationships on a solid foundation of true love. From that starting point, your romantic flow will carry you as you evolve higher and higher—within your partnerships and within yourself.

We are all our own greatest loves. Far from being narcissistic or self-centered, understanding how important self-love is makes you *more* loving toward others, not less. When you establish a boundary with someone who doesn't value you or your time, that boundary is in both of your highest good. Whether they agree isn't the point. They have their own love lessons to learn, just like you.

So it goes, each of us learning from each other in relationship with one another. Some of these lessons are unavoidably painful. But they all have meaning that you can use to grow in your skill at love. As you continue to navigate this adventure, be sure to keep love front and center as your destination and strategy. Don't let fear slam on the brakes; turn the car around and drive in the opposite direction. When you need a break, pull over. When you need a new vantage point, find it. Develop your own self-care superpowers so you can handle what comes with grace and ease.

Mindset, Heartset, Soulset, Skillset

The people meeting their soulmates and the ones meeting shallow partners or no one at all don't have the same beliefs about love. It seems obvious now, but I only discovered this truth thanks to my active participation in many other people's love journeys. It's easy to look at the happiest couples you know and think that the relationship itself is what empowered them to feel good about love. If you look closer, you'll see that most of the time it was their empowerment that led them to happiness. This is especially so when people intentionally set out to find true love. In other words, their love confidence enabled them to form a happy relationship, not the other way around. These are the ones who made their own luck in love, just as you're in the process of doing by reading this book.

By contrast, hoping to get lucky is a disempowered approach to true love that requires prolonged mental and emotional effort to convince oneself it'll happen. Somehow. Maybe. Hopefully. The inherent problem with that approach is you don't have to work to convince yourself of anything you truly believe. A push-pull of hope and doubt in love and dating is normal, but also counterproductive. Love doesn't flourish in our futile attempts to eradicate doubt. Redirecting yourself toward the love end of the doubt–certainty spectrum is always possible, even in the face of frustration or confusion. Your journey is calling you to more love, deeper love, higher love. If not, you wouldn't still be reading this book. Nurture that part of you that already knows your desire for true love is far more than a hope—it's a vision of what's to come.

how to find true love

Everything you've learned in this book about the mindset, heart-set, soulset, and skillset of true love will guide you toward aligning your power with the relationship you've already begun to create. We discussed in chapter 6 the paradoxical way deeply held fearful beliefs often manifest in precisely what you don't want. As you continue to grow on your love journey, self-compassion will always be there to assist you in transcending this paradox. It will give you the strength to reject the fear and perfectionism that blocks love.

Only by developing the self-awareness to know that how and what you think, feel, and believe about love matters can you reliably shift your romantic reality. Better to be self-aware and "bad" at dating (for now) than to falsely believe your skill at seduction alone will lead to true love. Being self-aware requires a loving humility about your own complexity and understanding that growth is your ultimate love assignment.

With your newfound knowledge of how to have a deeper connection with yourself, you can see yourself more clearly. Plus there's the added benefit of better understanding and honoring those you date and partner with. Love thrives in your life when you take others' capacity to co-create love less personally. When you release the expectation of the fairy-tale ideal of effortless partnership, you save yourself the distraction of trying to avoid your own love lessons. Because it's not always so easy out there in modern dating land, your choice to rise above the chaos will be put to the test. For any moments where you lose clarity and backslide into fear, don't panic. Remember you have an inner power to choose love, again and again. Your heart will grow braver and more skilled at love as you go.

You already have a fresh perspective on your thoughts about love, your feelings about yourself when it comes to love, and your connection to the higher love available to assist you. Combined with the foundational dating and connection skills you've learned in the final step of this book, you have more than enough knowledge of how to proceed. Remember that perfection isn't required and the universe will support you if you allow it to.

Create a 3-Month Dating Action Plan

What's working well in your dating life, and what's working less well? What would you rather your love life look like? With self-compassionate curiosity, ask yourself the following questions to get clear on what aligned action looks like for you in the coming months. Your answers will paint a clear picture of your next best steps.

1. How would I describe where I am today in this chapter of my dating journey?
2. How would I describe where I am today on my larger love journey?
3. What would I *love* for my romantic life to look like 3 months from now?
4. What, if any, obstacles do I foresee to making my 3-month vision a reality?
5. What would I have to do differently that's in *my department* to achieve that three-month vision?
6. What intention(s) will I set to assist me in getting there with as much ease as possible?
7. What's the most courageous step I could take right now in the direction of true love?
8. Do I have a dating self-care plan? What is it?
9. What steps will I take to center love in my life more holistically?

Some Final Dating Advice

#1: Timing

By now I hope you've gained a new level of clarity and insight about your romantic life. As you move forward, use the Dating Action Plan questions in the previous section to help you commit to some tangible goals. Set yourself up to win—don't aim to be in a true love partnership in three months if you're currently just beginning to date and discover your love confidence. You may exceed your goals, because the universe is abundant and windfalls of love happen every day. True love is worth the wait; also, releasing the urge to control the timing of it clears the resistance that impatience can cause. For now, balance pushing yourself out of your comfort zone with expecting a 180-degree turnaround overnight. It could happen, though—and if that's what you want, your commitment to *doing* love should reflect that desire.

As you're dating and meeting new people, trying on new flirting styles, and choosing love over fear, you'll get feedback. It'll show up in your thoughts and emotions and your attractions. Give yourself permission to pause and shift your perspective when you feel any disconnection from the energy of love. If dating feels hopeless or frustrating, remember your power to change *how* you're dating, and who. Most importantly, remember that you are your own destiny. Finding true love within will reveal that it was hiding in plain sight. Like Dorothy in *The Wizard of Oz*, you had the power within you all along.

#2: Develop Your Authentic Flirting Style

In chapter 13, you learned all about the styles and purposes of flirting. Those are the basics. The next step is to put your own unique spin on how you best flirt. Discovering that is how you unleash your most magnetic and captivating self.

Some questions to help you develop your authentic flirting style:

1. What's most effective given your love goals? (e.g., if you're prioritizing someone's character or readiness for commitment, relying on physical touch to flirt might not convey that as effectively as attentiveness.)
2. What's the most natural, given your personality? (e.g., playful banter might be your sweet spot in flirting if it fits how you like to interact with others.)
3. What makes *you* feel seen, special, and acknowledged? (That's a great place to start in your flirting experiments.)
4. What can you do to feel more confident and magnetic energetically? (e.g., balancing effort and pressure about your appearance, spending time in places where you feel more at ease and inspired.)

Perfect isn't the goal, prepared is. Have fun with expanding your comfort to give and receive more love.

#3: The Wider Dating Pool

Perhaps you're only open to romantic involvement with people of certain races, religions, or backgrounds. A client once said, "Being with a Black, Christian man is my heart's desire. It's the only thing I'm open to." For my client, herself Black and Christian, this was her truth and the only kind of person she'd ever been attracted to, despite knowing people of many different backgrounds. If you feel similarly convicted to only be with someone of a particular group, that is of course your choice to make.

However, the reason why you've made that choice is worth examining. Like my client said, it's her heart's desire. For many people their "why" is attraction, or raising children with a certain belief system or within a particular community. I never push back on clients when they give answers like that, because they are clear in their motivation for making that choice. But on the question of being open to dating other groups, I often hear assumptions, not conviction. Here are some common ones that keep people from opening themselves to new possibility:

- *They* don't want to date someone like me.
- I don't have anything in common with *them*.
- No one from any other group has ever approached me.

I give a little nudge on these answers because they're not about heart's desire. They're beliefs that may or may not be true or even desired to be true. Would you be open to dating someone from a different background for the first time? How about if you found them interesting, attractive, and aligned with your values? There's no population of people who are uniformly the right match for you, and that includes any community you belong to or group identity you share. So perhaps allowing yourself to be surprised by those of different groups is in fact in your highest good.

#4: Co-creating Chemistry

Most people chase romantic chemistry instead of seeing themselves as co-creators of it. "Liking someone as a friend" doesn't mean you don't have chemistry; it just means it's not romantic. In both cases, a bond was formed. This often happens when you start dating available people. Sometimes a friendship bond catches on fire with romantic passion. Matchmakers look to set up people who are open to *generating* chemistry, knowing it might grow into more. There's simply no guarantee that any two people will have romantic chemistry, no matter how much they are each other's "type." And sometimes—maybe even a lot of the time—you don't see chemistry coming, but still it arrives as an unexpected surprise. Experienced matchmakers will tell you that anyone who says "I know within the first two minutes if we're a match" is not someone you're likely to have success matching.

My advice is be open to exploring chemistry. I don't advocate dating someone for months (much less years) without having romantic chemistry. But I do encourage you to lean in and explore the possibility as you're getting to know someone new. Chances are you've met at least one person in the past who you weren't attracted to until that day when things shifted. Perhaps it was when you started to discover things about them that you liked, or because getting to know each other without the pressure of expectation freed you both up to be your authentic selves. That's where genuine chemistry can blossom and thrive. You empower yourself in a very significant way when you acknowledge that you're a chemistry generator, not just a recipient. Be open to leaning in, using your flirting skills, and see if you can move the needle in the direction of romantic chemistry when you meet someone who otherwise seems like a good potential match. You might find yourself very grateful that you did.

#5: When Things Don't Work Out

Sometimes, of course, things don't work out. Or rather, relationships end, relationships never get a chance to begin, trust is broken, or your connection is lost. As I've mentioned elsewhere throughout this book, I encourage you to always find the meaning in your relationships. Your disagreements and pain points are lessons. Learn from how they end, and why they end. Did the breakup show you how overdue the split actually was? How might you do better next time? Are you able to forgive? To be accountable for your role in an untenable dynamic?

The best we can do is to be compassionate, be responsible for our choices, and keep returning to love. Remember that no matter how dire it might seem at times, you'll never run out of love or chances at true love.

One Last Time . . .

Before you go, I want to remind you one last time of a key lesson from each part of this book:

Self-compassion is your best friend (MINDSET): Life, as you've undoubtedly noticed, is not easy. What makes it a *lot* easier, however, is being kind to yourself. The shame fog that we can get trapped in doesn't benefit you or anyone else. Use self-compassionate curiosity to provide relief whenever you can't see the way forward. Kindness is often your next best step.

How you see yourself is how you'll see yourself (HEART-SET): If you were convinced (falsely, I might add) that you're unlovable, you wouldn't be able to allow yourself the experience of being loved. Even when people truly do love you. Remember that fear can only be transcended through the power of love, which includes knowing yourself. Use the self-love check-in and revisit your love beliefs to strengthen your belief in how worthy you truly are of the love you want.

Stick to your department by relying on the universe (SOUL-SET): Don't, as my friend Angela says, try to "be" the law of attraction. You are not in charge of the universe; you're only in charge of yourself. Thank goodness! That alone is a full-time job. Let go of the reins and step into the loving energy of trust. Cooperate with the universe and do your part to find true love through the power of intention, gratitude, surrender, and serendipity. The universe will do the rest to bring you together with the right people.

Dating skills are love skills (SKILLSET): Remember the purpose of this lifelong love journey you're on. You are destined to grow in your skill at giving, receiving, and embodying the energy of love. Stay empowered and know you always have romantic agency and opportunity waiting for you to discover. The next time you meet someone wonderful, observe all the ways in which love is an inside job. Dating (and your true love relationship) is where self-love and romantic love collide—pay attention to both.

Be Lovingly Courageous

Hopefully you feel more confident now than you did when you began this book. I hope you continue on the path to true love with a renewed energy and commitment to expanding the love within. Keep your heart open. Help your friends on their adventures by demystifying the dating process and spreading the word that we can all do better when it comes to romantic love. Dating culture changes when enough people hold themselves to a higher standard of love and connection. And that begins with you.

If necessary, let your desire for romantic love be your motivation for self-love. That works! It's a huge motivator for a reason. You didn't choose your desire for loving partnerships (romantic or otherwise) any more than you chose your desire for oxygen. Like the air we breathe, love is a default setting of being human because it matters to our existence. Keep self-love as the essential starting point. Set the most loving version of yourself as your ultimate destination. With that intention, you are well-equipped to grow in love every single day.

Love is the opposite of fear. Let it give you courage—it has plenty for us all. Sometimes courage is striking up a conversation, telling someone how you really feel, or going on a blind date. At other times, courage is saying no, prioritizing self-care, or asking yourself a tough question. Let love, courage, and romantic possibility surprise you with their depths. You've got this.

Heartwork

1. Write down the following: Based on what I've learned in this book, what perspective, tools, or guidance do I want to be sure to remember when it comes to my love journey?

   - Mindset
   - Heartset
   - Soulset
   - Skillset

2. Write yourself a love letter. Use the self-love check-in from chapter 4 as a guide if necessary. Tell yourself what you most need to hear about how amazing and lovable you truly are!

   You've done a wonderful job. I am so proud of you and I hope you're proud of you too. I wish you a life full of true love. You deserve nothing less.

Acknowledgments

The road to this book can be directly traced back to my Bronx childhood. I was born with the greatest of fortunes—a loving family. Growing up, I had two parents who truly loved each other and demonstrated it daily, in words and actions. Unconditional respect, which I now understand to be a key pillar of true love, was the default setting in our family. Disagreements naturally happened, but a lack of basic kindness did not. Credit for whatever wisdom I have about how to be loving belongs first and foremost to my parents, Joyce and Edward Hogi. Long before I ever had my first boyfriend, my father regularly schooled me on the importance of picking partners who had strong character. His great advice to me—to pay attention not only to how someone treats you, but how they treat others—has protected me in countless ways. It was my mother who highlighted that the way a person thinks will tell you everything you need to know about the kind of choices they'll make. You both taught me gratitude and faith in something greater than myself. Thank you for being the blueprint, and for liking me as well as loving me. I love you more than I can say.

No one—and I mean no one—has ever had kinder siblings than mine: Jana King and Marc Hogi. Thank you, sister, for the unending guidance, generosity, and encouragement throughout my entire life. I love you. To my brother, Marc—having an older brother who only ever protected me is one of the greatest blessings of my life. To my grandmothers, Minnie Pruitt King and Hortencia Vidal Hogi, if you were born today you'd be running the world. I'm in awe of your badassness. My entire extended family has my love and gratitude. Thank you especially to my Uncle Bill (Ret. Col. William S. King) for recognizing and loving me for the things I thought made me weird and maybe unlovable.

To my father and brother—even in death you're still teaching me, and I suspect, protecting me as well.

There are so many people to thank for this book coming to fruition. Many thanks to Paul C. Brunson, for not only inspiring my entire career path, but also for mentoring me along the way. A special thank-you to Simon Sinek for being the one to tell me to write this book. Your support and friendship mean the world to me. Thank you to my wonderful agents, Christy Fletcher, Kelly Karcewski, and the team at UTA. My undying gratitude goes to Nana Twumasi and the entire team at GCP Balance, including Natalie Bautista, Carrie Andrews, and cover designer Jim Datz. This book literally wouldn't exist without you. Thank you for taking a chance on me.

The TED community has been life-changing in all the best ways. Thank you to Kelly Stoetzel for bringing me into the fold. Many thanks as well to Cyndi Stivers, Raven White, Susan Zimmerman, and all the amazing TED humans I've been lucky enough to meet, collaborate with, be inspired by, and learn from.

Having author friends to commiserate with and learn from has been such a gift. Bevy Smith, thank you for everything! To Denise Hamilton—thank you for your support. Kathryn Finney, you are a rockstar. Thank you. Damona Hoffman, thank you for always telling it to me straight and being my coaching BFF. Aycee Brown, thank you for being my book-writing buddy. London Hughes, you're the only friend I ever made on a podcast! You are a such a light. Faith Childs Davis, thank you for extending my first-ever invitation (in 2008!) to write about dating and your encouragement throughout my book-writing process.

Thank you to D.O.M., who kept me safe and sane through the pandemic and gave me boundless support, encouragement, and love. I'm forever grateful. Thank you Erin and Reagan Stevens for being my sisters. Michael Coppock, thanks for letting me meddle in your love life for all these years. To my adopted sister, Helene Miller, and brother-in-law, James Kase, you are my forever family. To my godsons Sam, Jesse, Levi, and Kobe Kase: It brings me so much joy that you ask me for love advice, and even more that you take it. I'm so proud of you and I love you so much. Thank you Sheri Robertson for being my second big sister and for bringing Clay, Andrew, Sydney, and E into this world. To my youngest godchild, Zora Beverly—you're too young for this book right now, but one day I will stick my nose in your love life, too. I love you!

To my Australian twin, Felicity Fellows—thank you for being my confidante and for holding my hand as I wrote this book. I can't wait for our next adventure. Bruno Giussani, there's too much to say here. Thank you for getting me to the finish line of this book, believing in me, and so much more.

My endlessly wonderful friends include Louisa Brown, Colin Appiah, Erika Lewis, Suzanne Hollingshead, Eliza Orlins, Adia Millett, Alaina Beverly, Jojo Rodriguez, Trinity Bailey, Kailani Bayot, Jodine Dorce, Patty Song Lee, Gina Bieber, VP Walling, Corinne Kaplan, Michele Pore, Oceans Six, Wine and Cheese, WAWG, and many more. I am truly the luckiest person. I couldn't dream of better friends to do life with.

Finally, my deepest gratitude goes to my clients and students. You have inspired me and taught me more about true love than I ever thought possible. I didn't even know what I didn't know until you trusted me to play a role in your love journeys. Without your vulnerability, trust, resilience, and courage, I never could have written this book. You have my heart and gratitude forever. May you always have an abundance of true love.